DEAD ON ARRIVAL
IN MANHATTAN

DEAD ON ARRIVAL
IN MANHATTAN

Stories of Unnatural Demise
from the Past Century

LAWRENCE R. SAMUEL

THE
History
PRESS

Published by The History Press
Charleston, SC
www.historypress.com

First published 2021

Manufactured in the United States

ISBN 9781467147262

Library of Congress Control Number: 2021934128

CONTENTS

PREFACE

arriage rides through Central Park. Shopping on Fifth Avenue. A Broadway matinee. You'll find no mention of such cheery experiences here. Rather, this book is about the dark side of life in Manhattan, a side of life that has one thing in common: death. *Dead on Arrival in Manhattan* reveals the ugly underbelly of the city so nice they named it twice, the kind of things that we usually don't like to think about. Murder, suicide and other unnatural deaths of a surprisingly wide variety fill these pages, reminding us that for some folks, life just doesn't end well. With so many people packed into a relatively small space, it's understandable how the island seems to have had more than its share of such stories, reason enough to revisit them in all their gruesome detail.

Dead on Arrival in Manhattan is a wild and often disturbing ride through the history of what many people agree is the greatest city in the world. Unlike most "official" histories of Manhattan, however, this one is not interested in the financial triumphs, creative breakthroughs or other remarkable achievements that have come to define the borough and its residents. This more unofficial history tells the stories of ordinary individuals who, for some reason or another, died suddenly and often violently. In some ways, it's a more accurate or representative history of life in Gotham, as it is not concerned with greatness of any sort. "There are eight million stories in the naked city," went a line in an old television show about crime in New York City, words that speak for the premise of this book. *Dead on Arrival in Manhattan* tells some of those millions of stories, offering a glimpse into the lives of people who shared the single, sad fate of being pronounced dead on arrival.

To that point, while this book focuses on the death of certain individuals, it is really about the circumstances that were in play at that final and unfortunate point in their respective lives. What were the reasons for one spouse finding his or her gun and shooting the other dead? Why did young men and women, seemingly in the prime of their lives, decide to kill themselves? How did some individuals actually die, the complete facts mysteriously cloaked in the reporting? It is such questions lurking behind the deaths that I find most interesting, as the possible answers tell us something about the strange directions that the course of life can take any of us. I understand how many people might find these stories morbid, but I find them fascinating slices of life and an integral part of the usually untold history of Manhattan.

Dead on Arrival in Manhattan relies exclusively on the published accounts of those stalwart reporters who covered the local murder and suicide beat, staples of newspaper journalism in the first half of the twentieth century. With regard to the latter, reports of "jumpers" were regularly featured in newspapers through the 1960s, after which editors chose not to cover them for fear that doing so would encourage copycat suicides. For the sake of accuracy and as a matter of respect for the protagonists in the stories, the book sticks closely to the facts gathered for newspaper articles. Additionally, the material in *Dead on Arrival in Manhattan* dates back at least fifty years, another means of showing consideration for those whose lives ended tragically and for anyone who may have known them.

In many ways, the Manhattan of a half century to a century ago would be unrecognizable today. The borough has always been perceived as a place that is not reluctant to destroy the old in order to create the new, something that has been especially true through much of the twentieth century. Fifty to one hundred years of "progress" have transformed the physical and cultural landscape of the island to such a degree that a trip back in time would be a generally alien experience. One looking for the Javits Center or the Time Warner Center, for example, would not find either; beginning in 1956, the city's major exhibition hall was the New York Coliseum, located where the Time Warner Center is today. The Madison Square Garden erected in 1925 was then located on 50th Street and 8th Avenue; it would be demolished in 1968, and the new one on top of Penn Station opened that same year. Sadly, the original, magnificent Penn Station was razed in 1963.

Shopping too was a different animal in this era before the likes of national chain stores such as Gap, Banana Republic and Old Navy. At its inception in 1892, Abercrombie & Fitch was not a clothier for teens staffed by hunky young men and fit women but rather the best sporting goods store in the country. (Before the store sold jeans, tees and hoodies, it specialized in things like tents, canoes, fishing tackle and guns.) Department stores like Wanamaker's, B. Altman's, Gimbels, Abraham & Straus, Arnold Constable, Korvette's, Stern's, Bonwit Teller and Alexander's littered Manhattan before the age of specialty stores (and mergers and acquisitions) kicked in. Men flocked in droves to buy suits at Bond Clothing Stores, which was the nation's biggest clothier by the 1960s. Barney's, located on 7th Avenue between West 16th and West 17th Streets, was a discount retailer, selling suits for about sixty dollars.

Has anything not changed substantially in New York since 1970? Lots. Like now, Chinatown and Little Italy were ethnic potpourris of sights, sounds and smells and Harlem mostly African American. Lincoln Center, Carnegie Hall and Town Hall were very much around, although the New York City Ballet and New York City Opera have since moved. Broadway was still Broadway, with many theaters in the West 40s packing them in, and there was an off-Broadway scene as well. Washington Square Park, Union Square Park, Madison Square Park, Bryant Park, Riverside Park and, of course, Central Park were then as now escapes from the urban madness, and Gramercy Park has always been private. Animals have lived happily at the Central Park Zoo since 1934 (and in a menagerie since 1864), and the United Nations, the Empire State Building and Chrysler Building were iconic structures just as they are now. The New York Public Library at 42nd Street and 5th Avenue (lions and all) has hardly changed a bit, and Grand Central Terminal was thankfully saved from the wrecking ball.

IMPORTANTLY, *DEAD ON ARRIVAL in Manhattan* features people who, save for their death, typically led rather ordinary lives. It is not about the demise of the famous, who I believe have already received more than their fair share of attention, and not exclusively about the shoot-em-ups associated with organized crime. I'm as big a fan as anyone of the accounts of gang hits taking place in Italian restaurants while nearby diners nibbled on their calamari and cannoli, and this book includes some, but such stories have overshadowed equally compelling of chronicles of abrupt death. What have not gotten their historical due are stories of regular Manhattanites (and, occasionally, visitors to the city) whose lives were suddenly and often unexpectedly snuffed out, something *Dead on Arrival in Manhattan* tries to rectify.

Given the subject matter, the stories in this book are windows into what must have been in many cases people living "lives of quiet desperation," as Thoreau described the plight of the majority. The stories speak for themselves, describing in plain but often painful detail who did what to whom. In some cases, we are given a reason or at least a hint why what took place did take place, but just as often we are left wanting more information. Reading between the lines is helpful in this regard, especially if we are provided with some clues. Imagining the full circumstances of each case by extrapolating from the facts provided is actually a big part of the book's appeal, I believe, although we will never really know how someone (or, in some cases, more than one person) ended up dead.

It's important to note that rather than being simply a collection of stories, *Dead on Arrival in Manhattan* offers readers a compelling narrative grounded in a number of central themes that are, whether we like it or not, universal to the human condition. Versus an anthology of disparate newspaper articles written by journalists, in other words, the stories are linked together by my exploration of the unfortunate but undeniably real-life themes of tragedy, violence, misfortune and sorrow. The stories are told chronologically and in my own voice, creating a disturbing yet fascinating narrative that reveals underexamined, less savory aspects of the human experience.

Of course, violent death can and does happen everywhere, but *Dead on Arrival in Manhattan* makes it clear that New York seems to have had more than its fair share. With a large, dense population, often crowded into small apartments, it isn't surprising that death has reared its ugly head when emotions got especially high or something went horribly wrong. As anyone who has lived there knows, Gotham can be a pressure cooker, particularly when money and/or sex is involved. Toss in a significant degree of verticalness and, in many situations, no air conditioning into the mix, and it's perhaps understandable how a couple of New York's finest along with a coroner ended up working overtime. Noir-like episodes much like those in films and pulp novels appear with regularity in this work, blurring the lines between art and life.

All of the episodes here at least appear to involve unnatural death, meaning the protagonists' lives were interrupted by some intervening factor that shortened their normal lifespans. Hotels comprise a surprising percentage of where the final moments of life occurred; both residents and visitors to Manhattan saw these places as a good place to die or kill someone due to the anonymity they offered. (Guests often registered with an assumed name and address, sometimes making it difficult for their bodies to be identified.) Characters throughout these stories were often described as "despondent" or having suffered from "nervous disorders" and "breakdowns." (Today some would likely be diagnosed as clinically depressed or bipolar and be prescribed medication.) Suicides tended to be unemployed, in bad financial straits, in poor health, suspected of a crime or part of a romance gone bad. (The 1929 market crash and subsequent Great Depression threw many lives into disarray.) Friends and family members routinely denied their loved one took their own lives, citing some other (much less likely) cause of death. There was (and remains) a stigma associated with suicide, and there could be the more practical matter of life insurance should the death be deemed an accident or murder. Weirdly, perhaps, the newly dead were frequently found in their pajamas, but upon reflection, this was probably as good as any way to go to whatever lies beyond this world.

The number of cases involving wealthy and successful people was surprising to me. Being pronounced dead on arrival was an equal opportunity occurrence, with membership in a privileged social or economic class or an Ivy League college degree no guarantee that one would make it to old age. There are many different ways to die, we learn in vivid detail. Not surprisingly, alcohol and drugs often entered the equation, and death seemed to spike around the holidays. Cooking gas accounts for a disproportionate amount of the cases, so much so that at some point the providers of the utility hired emergency crews to try to rescue those overcome by it, whether intentionally or otherwise. Bad liquor during Prohibition was another major killer, but I've avoided such stories, as they're just not very interesting. No victims under the age of eighteen are presented here, as such stories are just too sad, even for me, and I have not included deaths stemming from automobile crashes or fires.

To that point, the stranger the better when it comes to retrieving this kind of material from the dustbin of history. One couldn't make these stories up, and they demonstrate that truth really is stranger than fiction. Unlike the plots in many TV shows and movies, these are entirely real and clearly illustrate life's rich banquet. (The material can, however, serve as inspirational fodder for a screenwriter drawing on true events "ripped from the headlines.") The stories rarely made the front page of newspapers, often hidden in the back alongside other goings-on in the city, state, nation or world considered relatively unimportant. In a certain sense, however, they were important, encapsulating in just a few paragraphs the sweep of an individual's life.

Rather than being exploitive, I see these stories as a tribute of sorts and a means of offering a kind of immortality to those who met an untimely end and would likely otherwise be forgotten. In each vignette, we learn something about the individual's life, something that is typically at least as interesting as his or her death. With just a few exceptions, the newspaper reports carried no bylines, so I'm indebted to those journalists of the past who covered the dead-on-arrival beat. Again, I'm not interested in solving crimes, if there was one, or trying to figure out why someone decided to take his or her life. I leave that up to you, and readers are welcome to search for material that may provide closure in such matters.

If there is one takeaway from this book, it's that death reared its ugly head all over Manhattan during these years, with every neighborhood having its share of dead on arrivals. Bad guys were seemingly everywhere, disproving the popular notion that life in the Big Apple was kinder and gentler decades ago. We tend to look back at the past as a more innocent and happier time, but these pages stand as hard evidence that this was not the case. If anything, Manhattan appeared to be a scarier place a half century or century ago, providing some sense of comfort to those of us who are privileged to call it home.

Enjoy your visit to Gotham's darker side.

1
THE 1920s

To put it mildly, Manhattan in the Roaring Twenties was an exciting place to be. It was the Jazz Age, of course, so that music could be heard at any number of the speakeasies that popped up when Prohibition began in 1920. Radio was all the rage, and orchestras led by Fletcher Henderson, Paul Whiteman and Duke Ellington were based in Manhattan. Flappers really did the Charleston, and Tin Pan Alley (located on West 28th Street between 6th Avenue and Broadway) remained the source of much of the music Americans listened to throughout the decade.

There were many other amusements to be had in Manhattan during the 1920s, and the booming economy allowed all social classes to enjoy much of it. Movie houses clustered around Times Square became increasingly popular as vaudeville declined, and Broadway shows, especially the Ziegfeld Follies, were packing them in. Considerable "high" culture could also be found on all parts of the island, ranging from the downtown musings of Greenwich Village bohemians to the witty work of the Algonquin Round Table in midtown and the exploding arts scene that was taking place uptown in Harlem. Taking the subway or one's brand-new Model T to see the Yankees in the Bronx or to the beach at Coney Island in Brooklyn were also popular pastimes.

Against this pleasant backdrop, however, was a cultural climate that allowed crimes of all sorts to flourish. Prohibition opened the floodgates for gads of illegal cash to be made, and organized crime rushed in to take full advantage of the law. Bootlegging emerged as a primary business among

Poster for a revue of music from Tin Pan Alley. *Sommese, Lanny, Artist. Tin Pan Alley–A Revue of Popular Music. None. [University park, pa: penn state university, between 1980 and 1990] Photograph. https://www.loc.gov/item/2015647913/.*

Times Square at night, 1921. *The Miriam and Ira D. Wallach Division of Art, Prints and Photographs: Picture Collection, The New York Public Library. "Times Square North: Night Illumination." New York Public Library Digital Collections. Accessed March 27, 2020. http:// digitalcollections.nypl.org/items/510d47e1-0689-a3d9-e040-e00a18064a99.*

gangsters based in the Lower East Side or Little Italy, and widespread political corruption that was tolerated if not sponsored by Tammany Hall provided a breeding ground for various forms of racketeering. With so much money at stake, was it any surprise that so many residents of and visitors to Manhattan ended up dead on arrival? If that were not enough, the pressures of modern life were taking a toll on some Manhattanites, leading to numerous other cases of unnatural death.

THE SILK MERCHANT

Much confusion surrounded the death of Isaac Mendelson, a "wealthy silk merchant," who died in his office on East 23rd Street in October 1920. Mendelson's fortunes had recently changed for the worse, however, as he had lost a whopping $2 million (about $26 million today) on a silk deal. A pair of private detectives on patrol in the office building discovered Mendelson's body and the man's safe open, leading them to think he had been robbed and murdered. Witnesses seeing two men running in the stairwell made the detectives that much more convinced that a dastardly deed had taken place, and a homicide squad was promptly dispatched from the local police headquarters.[1]

Upon the arrival of a Dr. Thompson from Bellevue Hospital, however, the murder theory was soon dismissed. Thompson noticed that Mendelson's lips were stained, a common sign of the victim having drunk a poisonous liquid. Sure enough, a bottle and a glass containing Lysol, the cleaning product, was discovered lying near the corpse. Suicide was the cause of death, agreed Dr. Charles Norris, chief medical examiner, the recent financial disaster

Bellevue Hospital. *Fellheimer & Wagner, Client, Gottscho-Schleisner, Inc, photographer. Bellevue Hospital, 28th St., New York City. View from outpatient's room IA. New York New York State New York. United States, 1950. Aug. 4. Photograph. https://www.loc.gov/item/2018723640/.*

no doubt the reason why the once wealthy silk merchant took his own life. Two notes were subsequently found, confirming the cause of death. "If something happens to me notify my wife," read one, the other bequeathing the $340 in his desk drawer (perhaps his sole remaining funds) to his family.[2]

THE CRYSTAL CHANDELIER

The relative tranquility of the Upper West Side was certainly disrupted in May 1921 when William Becker arrived at the apartment of his former wife, now a Mrs. Miller. Becker, a forty-year-old electrical engineer, had frequently shown up unannounced at the apartment on West 87th Street since he and his wife divorced seven years earlier. This time, however, the man was clearly intoxicated, and when told by his wife that their son was not present, he became enraged. Furniture was thrown about, and in his violent state, Becker accidently slashed his right wrist on the crystal chandelier in the dining room. Blood gushed out of the man's arm, prompting Mrs. Miller and her maid to run out the room.[3]

Woozy from his loss of blood, not to mention the high level of alcohol in his system, Becker proceeded to one of the bedrooms, where he lay down. When the maid checked on him three hours later (to see if he wanted to join Mrs. Miller for dinner, oddly enough), she found the bed soaked with blood and Becker apparently dead. A local doctor was called; he pronounced Becker dead at the scene and summoned the police. She divorced Becker after such ugly, alcohol-infused episodes, Mrs. Miller told Detective Golding and Chief Medical Examiner Norris, and his drinking had greatly intensified over the past few weeks. Indeed, Becker's heart was about to give out anyway, Norris determined, this latest binge compounded by his unfortunate confrontation with the chandelier.[4]

A MODE OF DEATH

Many suicides are impulsive acts and have something to do with depression, but that certainly wasn't the case for fifty-four-year-old Thomas Collins, who shot himself in May 1921 in his apartment on East 79th Street. Having little money and no family and in poor health, Collins made a conscious choice to take his own life on a specific day and even at a specific time (3:30 a.m.). Collins was a retired dental surgeon and a graduate of the University of Chicago but had fallen on hard times.[5]

His plan set, the man sent letters to a number of acquaintances informing them that by the time they received the notes, he would be dead. One such letter was sent to the Reverend Dr. John Haynes Holmes, pastor of the Community Church, which Collins occasionally attended. Collins had recently asked Holmes if the church could cover the costs of his funeral, a request to which the latter had agreed. Collins had also left a suicide note making it clear that the impending gunshot was self-inflicted and that he was fully aware of what he was about to do. "It is a mode of death which I long since set for myself," he wrote, proceeding to carry out his wish at precisely the time he had planned.[6]

A FOURTEEN-INCH KNIFE

Could a person pull a fourteen-inch knife out of his chest after being stabbed while sleeping? That's exactly what appeared to have taken place in May 1921 when Giovanni Aresca died in his apartment on West 30th Street. The thirty-six-year-old Aresca had previously served as the chef on the steamer *Manchuria*, but he was now engaged in some kind of enterprise involving significant numbers of men and women visiting the apartment at all hours of the day and night. The knife that killed Aresca was so long and propelled with such force that it went clear through his back after entering his chest, but that apparently did not stop the dying man from somehow extracting it from his body after getting out of his bed.[7]

How did the police and detectives come to such an unlikely conclusion? The blade lay beside the punctured Aresca when a neighbor literally stumbled over the man's body, partly wrapped in a sheet and lying in a hallway. Investigators at the scene were amazed that anyone could perform such a feat and also surprised to find a considerable sum of money in the apartment, ruling out robbery as the motive. A bald man had run out of the tenement house around 1:30 a.m., a milkman later told police, but what had transpired in the wee hours of the morning to trigger such a bloody scene remained unclear.[8]

THE RIGHT STOCKING

Mrs. Adam Chelep's peculiar habit of keeping her life savings in her right stocking would cost the thirty-year-old resident of Avenue A her life in June 1921. (Wives often went by their husbands' first names at the time.) After returning from work, Mr. Chelep, a porter, found his wife dead, her right stocking torn and missing the $1,000 that she routinely kept in it. A chloroform-soaked handkerchief lay near Chelep's body, sufficient evidence for a policeman to declare that that was the cause of death.[9]

Policeman McDonald of the East 22nd Street Station also observed that Mrs. Chelep had likely struggled mightily with the thief. The position of the woman's body suggested that a fight had ensued (her right arm was extended over her head), and her fingers still clutched a clump of dark hair. No tenant had observed any strangers entering or leaving the building, leading detectives to bring the woman's sister and brother-in-law to the station for questioning. An autopsy and chemical analysis of the handkerchief were also planned to help catch the murderer and thief.[10]

THE GINGHAM APRON

It was not a pretty sight when Vera Tancrz entered her Chrystie Street apartment to find her landlady dead in July 1921. Fifty-seven-year-old Anna Koskovich (described as "elderly" by a newspaper reporter, something understandable given that life expectancy for American women was sixty-two at the time) was sprawled face-down on her bed, leaving no doubt that she had been murdered. Koskovich's arms were tied above her head with a towel, her mouth and nose were covered tightly by another towel and a gingham apron bound her ankles. Two irons sat on hot burners in the kitchen (a means of heating up the appliance before electric versions were commonplace), suggesting that Koskovich had been interrupted when her murderer entered the apartment.[11]

Tancrz, who along with a couple of others rented rooms in the apartment from Koskovich, ran screaming into the street after witnessing the terrible scene. A neighbor contacted the police, who in turn called a doctor from Gouverneur Hospital who concluded that Koskovich had suffocated and been dead for some time. No robbery or struggle had taken place, detectives determined, raising the question of why Koskovich was murdered and in such a brutal way. Fortunately, Tancrz had some answers. Her landlady often had a considerable amount of cash on the premises, specifically rent monies that would soon be deposited in the bank. Apparently believing that was the case, the slayer was no doubt disappointed to discover that no such prize was to be had that particular day. Koskovich had deposited the rent money the previous week, Tancrz informed the detectives, something the murderer had little way of knowing. Koskovich had recently been drinking with two male visitors, Tancrz added, making the pair the leading suspects until more information was gathered.[12]

THE WRONGS YOU HAVE DONE ME

A few months later and just a block away from that grisly scene, thirty-five-year-old Mae Jordan took her life by ingesting some kind of poison. Mrs. Jordan had divorced her physician husband, Dr. William Rosebaum, a year earlier and rather suddenly found herself in dire financial straits while living in her luxurious apartment at Broadway and West 86th Street. Jordan had not answered repeated phone calls over a period of days, a good friend told the building's superintendent, reason enough for the latter to enter her apartment with a spare key. Mrs. Jordan was dead in her bathroom, the super discovered, with the police called to investigate.[13]

Dr. Benjamin Schwartz, acting chief medical examiner, arrived on the scene and cited the cause of death as poison that Mrs. Jordan had swallowed about six days earlier. A note addressed to her ex-husband was found ("Dear Will," it began), confirming the suicide. Mrs. Jordan was behind in her rent, she explained, and asked her ex for $3,000 lest she be evicted. "Your neglect and the wrongs you have done me were the reasons I divorced you," Jordan wrote, but apparently, she decided to do herself in before sending the note. Mrs. Jordan was true to her word regarding her lowly pecuniary status. A search of her apartment revealed she possessed $5 in cash and some jewelry valued at about $1,500, clearly not enough to continue the lifestyle to which she was accustomed.[14]

WEDDING DAY

In November 1921, nineteen-year-old Harry Cook was shot dead in a deli where he worked on St. Mark's Place, the event made even more tragic by the fact that he was going to get married that day. Two policemen who happened to be on the street at that time actually saw Cook stagger out of the store and then fall dead with a bullet in his heart. Strangely, however, neither the policemen nor anyone else in the area had heard a shot or observed a possible shooter, making detectives wonder how the thing could have taken place. No gun was found on the scene, ruling out suicide as the cause of death. Had a rival for Cook's fiancée somehow shot the groom-to-be from a long distance and in a silent manner? The theory was a literal long shot, but no other motive was readily apparent.[15]

If the killing of Cook was strange, the circumstances surrounding it were equally odd and, it could be said, Shakespearean in plot. Cook's father objected to the marriage, it was learned, while the father of the bride-to-be had previously promised to give $400 to the owner of the store to make Cook a partner in the business. Cook had reportedly just learned that his future father-in-law threatened to withdraw his offer of $400 because he believed that Cook would not marry his daughter because of his father's objections. Could Cook's father or the father of his fiancée possibly have been the shooter? Nobody could say, making the case a particularly mysterious and heartbreaking one.[16]

GIVE ME A DRINK OF WATER

In March 1922, a Japanese man staggered into a cigar store in Chatham Square and handed twenty-eight dollars to a dumbfounded customer. "Give me a drink of water," the man said, dropping dead before getting his much-needed, expensive drink.[17]

Why so thirsty? The man had been shot through the abdomen and at close range, judging by the burn marks in his clothing where the bullet had entered. Many business owners in Chinatown were fiercely protective of their territory, especially against those of Japanese descent with aspirations to set up shop in the neighborhood. A culprit had yet to be caught, with police describing the hit simply as the result of a "feud."[18]

Chatham Square, circa 1905. *Detroit Publishing Co., Publisher. "L" Station, Chatham Square, New York. New York New York State New York. United States, 1905. [?] Photograph. https://www.loc.gov/ item/2016805354/.*

A BATTERED CANOE

In May 1922, sixty-four-year-old Dr. Frank Austin Roy, a notable physician and dental surgeon, was found dead in his apartment on West 33rd Street, a bullet wound through his right temple. Alerted by the man's sister that her brother was not showing up at his office on 5th Avenue, Patrolman Sullivan of the West 30th Street Station broke down the door to Roy's apartment. The partially clothed man was on his bed, a .38-caliber army revolver next to him.[19]

Why had the successful man ended his life? Friends of Roy told reporters that he had financial troubles, but there was much more to the story. A little over a year before, Roy's son, a dentist named Harold Roy, disappeared while crossing the Hudson River in a canoe. His battered canoe landed on shore at West 68th Street sans Roy, leading everyone to think that the man had drowned. The river was dragged, but no body was recovered, the logical conclusion being that the dead man's remains had drifted out to sea or much farther upriver. The Bankers' Life Insurance Company conceded that Roy was no more, granting his wife the full proceeds of his $10,000 policy.[20]

Many were thus expectedly shocked to hear the news a year later that Harold Roy was very much alive and living in Kansas City, none more so than his father, who was still in mourning over his son's presumed death. Soon after that, word came that the young Dr. Roy had opened a dentistry practice in San Francisco, and he had no intention of ever returning to New York City to happily reunite with his family and friends. The man had clearly faked his death and wanted a new and different life, begging the question of what was wrong with his old one. The trauma was seemingly too much for Harold's father, who ironically ended up being the actual dead Dr. Roy.[21]

AN ALARM CLOCK

One doesn't think of an alarm clock as a murder weapon, but that's exactly what it served as one nasty evening in August 1922. Leo Durnherr, a thirty-one-year-old salesman from a prominent Rochester family, was not at all happy to learn that his thirty-five-year-old wife planned to go to the funeral of her grandmother, who had just died in that city. Having imbibed heavily for days, Durnherr was in a particularly foul mood, and the news that his wife had every intention of heading upstate to say goodbye to her dead grandma put the man in a violent rage. Hearing a loud quarrel, a downstairs neighbor entered the couple's apartment on West 45th Street and told them to quiet down, which they did.[22]

The row soon started up again; however, there was soon total silence. Thinking that strange given the evening's earlier riotous proceedings, the neighbor went upstairs a couple of hours later to find the door of the apartment open. Mr. Durnherr was nowhere to be found, but his wife lay dead, a smashed alarm clock near her battered head. The glass of the clock was shattered, its metal case twisted and dented and the face so badly damaged that it could not be determined when the hands stopped moving.[23]

A Dr. Stoller from Flower Hospital, along with a pair of detectives from the West 47th Street Station, concluded that the alarm clock had to have been the murder weapon, and a search of the neighborhood was soon underway to locate the missing Durnherr.[24] The man was soon found sound asleep in a room at the Hotel Scarboro on West 43rd Street. His clothes and shoes were bloody, and when roused, he confessed to the gruesome crime.[25]

GET A JOB

In September 1922, Arthur Gintel of East 89th Street had just about enough of his wife's insistence that he "get a job" and stop living off her well-to-do parents' money. The couple had been married three years but was still living in her parents' apartment, a situation that Mrs. Gintel could no longer tolerate. Mr. Gintel had actually held a couple of jobs since their nuptials, but each one ended quickly, leading his wife to conclude that the man simply did not want to work.[26]

When his wife threatened to pursue a legal separation if he did not find another job and soon, Mr. Gintel chose a different course of action. The man chased Mrs. Gintel through her parents' apartment, overturning furniture, and cornered her in the kitchen, where he promptly cut her throat with a knife. Mr. Gintel wasn't done, however, stabbing himself ten times with the same knife he had just used to kill his wife. An ambulance soon arrived, but Mr. Gintel would not recover from his wounds.[27]

SOMETHING VERY QUEER

Something about the death of Dorothy King, a model, was "very queer," thought Chief Medical Examiner Norris when he viewed the woman's body in her apartment on West 57th Street in March 1923. The position of her body was unnatural, for one thing, and the empty bottle of chloroform on the floor near the bed left little doubt that King had met an unfortunate end. King, described by a reporter as "an unusually attractive blonde," was known in the neighborhood for the beautiful clothes and expensive-looking jewelry she routinely wore. No jewelry was found in her apartment, however, leading detectives to think that she had been robbed and murdered.[28]

Indeed, further investigation pointed to a low-level thief who was after King's furs and jewelry, specifically a bracelet of sapphires with a double row of small diamonds set in platinum, a ring with a pearl, a four-and-a-half-carat diamond ring, a pair of diamond earrings and a necklace with a two-carat sapphire. Planning to just knock King out, the thief exposed her to the chloroform for too long and accidentally killed her, police believed. Death would likely occur after inhaling chloroform for ten minutes, a doctor at Bellevue Hospital explained, and King was under for much longer than that. A group of men, led perhaps by King's former husband and known for befriending and then robbing women with expensive jewelry, was apparently behind the crime.[29]

ANOTHER ADMIRER

In August 1923, one hundred members of Congregation Minsk gathered for a service dedicated to President Warren G. Harding, who had recently died. In a hallway outside the synagogue, three shots rang out, one of them instantly killing twenty-year-old Louis Schwartzman with a bullet in the chest. Witnesses said that two men had walked up Rutgers Street, drew their revolvers and began firing at Schwartzman, narrowly missing his girlfriend, who was seated next to him. The gunmen ran a block to a taxi whose engine was already conveniently running. The cab sped away, its passengers likely delighted with their well-orchestrated hit.[30]

Hearing the shots, worshippers ran out of the synagogue, with one of them able to identify the dead young man. Fortunately, witnesses were able to describe the appearance of the pair of shooters in some detail and had also noted the number of the escape vehicle. Was Schwartzman involved in some kind of mob business given the nature of the assassination and the fact that Jewish gangsters were a ubiquitous presence on the Lower East Side at the time? Police did not think so, believing instead that another admirer of Schwartzman's girlfriend was responsible, making it a crime of passion. Tracing the taxi was an easy task, and police soon announced they knew the names of both the driver and the two hitmen.[31]

A PENNY ARCADE

In April 1924, a man walked into a penny arcade, which was a popular form of entertainment at the time that offered coin-operated games and activities.

One such activity at the arcade on East 14th Street was the shooting of clay pigeons with a rifle, a chance to test one's marksmanship. The man, a forty-five-year-old inventor named Monroe Sunshine, asked the attendant at the shooting gallery to load a .32-caliber pistol he had brought to the arcade. The attendant agreed, thinking that the man wanted to see how many pigeons he could hit with the gun. Instead, Sunshine fired a shot into his head and fell to the floor dead. The other patrons stopped whatever they were doing, naturally, and even the player piano grinded to a halt.[32]

What was behind Sunshine's odd choice of method to end his life? That wasn't clear, but it soon became evident that the man had a number of issues, including poor health and money problems, that led to his decision. His biggest demon, however, appeared to be an obsession with the various inventions he was working on. Sunshine was particularly fixated on how to create a postage stamp that didn't need to be licked, making him a man ahead of his time.[33]

THE FOLLIES GIRL

"Follies Girl Dies in Her Bathtub," declared a newspaper headline in August 1924, such a sensational story no doubt capturing many readers' attention. Indeed, the death of twenty-six-year-old Mary Warnock, a.k.a. Mary Julian, had all the ingredients that journalists live for. Julian was a Ziegfeld Follies chorus girl whose bruised and naked body lay in six inches of water in the bathtub of her apartment on West 95th Street. The woman should have been on stage at the New Amsterdam Theatre when her maid made the gruesome discovery, and she had never before missed a performance. Julian had come home alone the night before, it was learned, and had no visitors earlier in the day. Detectives were at a loss to explain how she died, wondering if foul play was involved, if she had a fatal heart attack as she was getting into the tub or if perhaps she had drowned. The story was as suspicious as they came, but more information was needed to determine the cause of death.[34]

Interviews with Julian's husband of five years (the couple was separated) and her sister provided some answers and perhaps solved the mystery. The young woman, who had been in New York for three years after arriving from Independence, Missouri, had a history of heart trouble. Just a year previously, in fact, Julian had been found unconscious in a bathtub, leading

Sheet music for "Swanee River Blues," a song from the 1923 Ziegfeld Follies. *Music Division, The New York Public Library. "Swanee River blues" New York Public Library Digital Collections. Accessed March 27, 2020. http://digitalcollections.nypl.org/items/510d47e3-f0e9-a3d9-e040-e00a18064a99.*

her doctor to predict that she would have an early death because of her cardiac condition. No poison or drugs were in her system, an autopsy revealed, and there was no evidence to suggest that she was murdered; however, questions remained.[35]

DEAR UMBERTO

It could be said that sixty-year-old Lesley Martin, a singing teacher, lived in a place most New Yorkers would covet, both now and in September 1925. Since 1905, not long after he arrived from New Zealand, Martin occupied a studio apartment in the Metropolitan Opera House located on Broadway between West 39th and West 40th Streets. (The building opened in 1883 after the original one burned down, and it stood until 1967.) Despite his envious digs, Martin was despondent and unwell, the reasons why he slashed his throat with a razor one afternoon.[36]

While leaving a note was and is quite common among those who take their own lives, it's rare for a suicide to stop midsentence. That's exactly what Martin did, however, unable to complete a letter he was writing to a friend while he made his fateful decision. "Dear Umberto," the letter began, telling Umberto Soccetti (a singer) that "everything is bad with me." "You know I was in the hospital and," were the final words in Martin's note, the prospect of even finishing the sentence apparently too much to bear for the man.[37]

Metropolitan Opera House, circa 1910. *The Miriam and Ira D. Wallach Division of Art, Prints and Photographs: Picture Collection, The New York Public Library.* "Metropolitan Opera House, New York, Which Seats 3200 Persons." *New York Public Library Digital Collections. Accessed March 27, 2020. http://digitalcollections.nypl.org/ items/510d47e0-d916-a3d9-e040- e00a18064a99.*

ELEVEN FINGERS

Six shots were fired from the doorway of a building on East 108th Street in September 1925, and Frank Guiffreda, who was better known in certain circles as "Eleven Fingers," was dead. Few mourned his loss, as the man's various occupations included thief, burglar, bootlegger, bookmaker and opium peddler. Mr. Eleven Fingers had crossed the wrong person, police believed, his slaying an act of revenge after some kind of crooked deal. (All six bullets were found in his body.) While no fewer than one hundred people had been in the area when the ambush took place, not one could describe the assailant, something not unusual when gangsters were involved. Even Guiffreda's wife, when informed of her husband's demise, refused to help the police find the killer, asking, "What good is it now he's dead?"[38]

Guiffreda's nickname was based on both biology and his penchant for taking things that did not belong to him. After the man was arrested for burglary a few years earlier, something that had taken place previously with considerable frequency, a detective coined the name, which stuck. Oddly enough, Guiffreda actually had an eleventh finger, a stubby thing located between his left hand's index finger and thumb. Apparently not fond of his sobriquet, Eleven Fingers had his extra one removed, but the surgery did nothing to stop others referring to him as such.[39]

A COAL SHOVEL

Another underworld character best known by his nickname was murdered a few months later and a few blocks away. Various rivals had previously fired gunshots at Ernest "Big" Fusco, a Harlem-based gambler, but unlike those directed at Eleven Fingers, no bullet ever connected. (Just a few weeks earlier, in fact, several shots were fired at him from a speeding automobile.) This time, in January 1926, a foe or foes chose a coal shovel to kill the thirty-year-old man, which had the desired effect. Mr. Big lay face-down on a coal pile in his brother's garage on East 105th Street, the murder weapon right beside his large body.[40]

Fusco's favorite form of gambling was craps (also referred to as just "dice"), and police believed he was playing that very game when he was struck with the shovel. Judging by the crossed position of the thumb and first finger on his right hand, detectives surmised, Big had just rolled the dice and was picking up his winnings when his skull was fractured. When the game started, Fusco had more than $1,000 in his pocket but none when his body was examined, his brother told police, making robbery the likely motive. Big was known for carrying large sums of money at all times, more evidence that he had been targeted for robbery. Arrested many times for gambling but never convicted, the man's luck had finally run out.[41]

THE KIBITZER

The Second Assembly District Democratic Club that was located at the Bowery and 4th Street hardly sounds like a likely place for a double murder. But such a crime did take place there in February 1926, when Red Russo and Patsy Griffo (both aliases) were shot dead during a card game. All of those who witnessed the act told police that a man known as "The Kibitzer" was responsible, and a search was on to find him. (Kibitzer is Yiddish for "a spectator offering advice or commentary, usually unwanted.")[42]

The Kibitzer was worthy of his moniker, often hovering around the table at which Russo, Griffo and other big-time gamblers played at the club. The man could not afford the high stakes at the table (his gambling budget was limited to two-dollar bets at the racetrack), but that didn't stop him from constantly looking at and remarking on the cards in the players' hands. "Shut up!" Griffo yelled at him that night, with Russo slapping the Kibitzer's face and ordering him out of the room when he would not remain quiet. The Kibitzer slunk away but soon reappeared, his hands now in his overcoat pockets. "You think you're tough?" he asked the men, pulling out a pistol and firing away before they had time to answer the question. Griffo tried to shoot back, but the Kibitzer fired another round at him. Griffo and Russo lay mortally wounded, while a third man named Larry Love was shot through his right cheek but survived.[43]

THE UNION MAN

As in many parts of the country between the world wars, New York City was a hotbed of strife between labor unions and company management. It was not unusual for disputes to become violent and in some cases end in

Fulton Street Fish Market, 1936. *The Miriam and Ira D. Wallach Division of Art, Prints and Photographs: Photography Collection, The New York Public Library. "Fulton Street Fish Market, Manhattan." New York Public Library Digital Collections. Accessed March 27, 2020. http:// digitalcollections.nypl.org/items/510d47d9-4f8d-a3d9-e040-e00a18064a99.*

fatality. Such was the case in May 1926, when the body of labor organizer William Mack was found riddled with bullets on Front Street near the Fulton Street Fish Market. A suspect was soon arrested, and detectives were able to determine where Mack had likely been shot four times before being dumped near the market. Mack had been at a nearby speakeasy, it was believed, his death the result of an ongoing feud between the United Sea Food Workers Union and local sellers of fish.[44]

Not coincidentally, perhaps, Mack was an officer of that union, making him a prime target for managers wanting to prevent their workers from becoming organized (and likely higher paid). This wasn't the first time that a union organizer was killed by people in the lucrative fish business. Just eight months earlier, in fact, an organizer named Maurice Britt was shot and killed, with fishmongers suspected of orchestrating that hit as well.[45]

CAT SAVES 8 LIVES

"Cat Saves 8 Lives," a cheery newspaper headline from April 1927 reads, the sadder news being that the feline apparently did not have the mythical nine lives. Coal gas from a furnace in the basement of a tenement house on Monroe Street had overcome the families living on the second floor, something that typically ended with fatalities. But a black-and-white cat came to the rescue, its loud meows waking up the sleeping residents. Windows were opened and police called, and Dr. Polimina of Gouverneur Hospital helped revive the woozy adults and children.[46]

The heroic feline was not as lucky, however, its tuxedo-like body found in the dining room of one the apartments. "Efforts to revive the animal were fruitless," the story ended, the brave creature pronounced dead on arrival.[47]

LAST RITES

The pistol fight that took place at the corner of West 14th Street and 9th Avenue in April 1927 seemed more Wild West than New York City. Two men approached each other from opposite directions and, when about thirty paces apart, whipped out their respective pistols and began firing. The duel undoubtedly had something to do with bootlegging, although the precise details of the dispute remained unknown when police arrived. What was clear was that Timothy Looman, a known bootlegger, was dead, and Thomas O'Brien, who had served as a gunman in the "Crybaby" robber gang, was wounded.[48]

Hopefully, the two men were better bootleggers than shots. About thirty bullets were fired between the two men, according to the many witnesses present, with just two finding their mark. After being shot, the wounded O'Brien was able to make his way about two hundred yards down 14th Street, where he collapsed directly in front of St. Bernard's Roman Catholic Church. Hearing the shootout, Monsignor Smith and Father Delaney exited their church and approached the fallen O'Brien, who still held his pistol. The men took the gun from O'Brien's hand and, seeing how badly he was wounded, administered last rites. Detectives pronounced Looman dead at the scene and took O'Brien to the prison ward of Bellevue Hospital, where he was charged

A Prohibition-era chemist for the Internal Revenue examining liquor to determine if it is "bootleg." *Treasury, Internal Rev. Chemist G.F. Beyer, 1920. Photograph. https://www.loc.gov/item/2016827376/.*

with murder. The two men had prearranged their gunfight, detectives learned, each of them likely knowing that just one would survive the public shootout.[49]

WHO SAYS SO?

Thirty-year-old Charles Donnelly was not at all happy to learn he would not get the steak he ordered in the dining room of the Machinery Club in the Hudson Terminal Building on Church Street. Steak was not on the menu that particular evening in July 1927, a waitress informed the man after checking in the kitchen. "Who says so?" Donnelly angrily asked, adding, "I'll fix that old bird," when told it was by order of Julius Teller, who was responsible for what was and what was not on the restaurant's menu. Donnelly, who worked at the cigar counter of the club, remained determined to get his piece of meat, marching into the kitchen, where he confronted Teller. Teller still refused to serve Donnelly the steak he desired, and the two men were

Postcard of the Hudson Terminal Building, 1914. *The Miriam and Ira D. Wallach Division of Art, Prints and Photographs: Picture Collection, The New York Public Library. "Hudson Terminal Building, New York" New York Public Library Digital Collections. Accessed March 27, 2020. http:// digitalcollections.nypl.org/items/510d47e2-8da3-a3d9-e040-e00a18064a99.*

soon exchanging fisticuffs. The headwaiter and other employees rushed to separate the men, and Donnelly returned to his table, where he reluctantly ordered something else.[50]

The story would have ended there if not for the fact that Teller did not fare as well in the scuffle as Donnelly. The seventy-year-old man lay nearly unconscious in the kitchen, reason enough for the headwaiter to call an ambulance from the Broad Street Hospital. Before a doctor arrived, however, Teller died, and Donnelly's meal was interrupted by police, who arrested the hungry man.[51]

SOMETHING POETIC

Premature deaths among young adults are always sad if not tragic, and Helen Oatman's was no exception. The nineteen-year-old, who resided with her parents and her brother, a student at Harvard, on West 93rd Street, appeared to have everything to live for. The woman had studied drama and art at the Miss Spence School and was currently enrolled at the New York School of Fine and Applied Arts, where she was studying music and philosophy. Oatman's family was well off, and she was known in society circles in both Philadelphia and Washington. She aspired to be a painter, but it was not to be.[52]

One night in July 1927, while her family was out of the apartment, Oatman took her own life by taking ether and then turning on the jets of a gas cooking stove. Upstairs neighbors found her body hours later when they smelled gas. She had left no note, but it was clear that the woman, whose short dark hair was very much in the flapper style of the day, had given considerable thought to her decision. Oatman bathed and then put on a new silk negligee that she had purchased for the special occasion. She laid a fresh linen sheet and several pillows on the kitchen floor near the stove. She then turned on all the jets and put her head in the oven, placing a dainty lace handkerchief soaked with ether near her face. An unfinished oil painting sat on an easel in an adjoining room, her palette and brushes on a nearby chair.[53]

Newspapers were filled with stories of suicides, but almost all of them mentioned financial ruin, illness or despondency as a motive. That was not the case for Oatman, and the young woman was not, as one might expect, moody or morose. (Her only notable quirk, if one could call it that, was a lack of interest in men.) Certainly odd, however, was her recently forged opinion that ending one's life was a rather lovely thing. After reading a newspaper report of a suicide a few days earlier, in fact, Oatman shared her thoughts on the subject with her mother, as the latter recalled soon after her daughter's death. "There is something poetic about suicide, something beautiful," she is said to have remarked, the wheels apparently set in motion.[54]

A .38-CALIBER LEAD BULLET

When twenty-seven-year-old Samuel Golden left his New Jersey home one morning in August 1927, there was no way for him to know that he would be involved in a high-speed car chase that day in Manhattan. He also could not know that it would be the last day of his life.[55]

All was well as he and a few friends drove down Columbus Avenue. Suddenly, at 59th Street, a roadster caromed off a pillar and struck Golden's car. Patrolman Michael Ledden witnessed the collision, leapt onto the running board of Golden's auto and ordered him to follow the roadster, which was traveling north. Golden did as he was told, but the roadster, driven by a James Morton (who had stolen the car, it turned out), was too fast. Morton was also zigzagging and occasionally driving on the sidewalk, making Ledden believe they would never catch him. The officer, thinking it was now or never, fired a few shots at the roadster, but missed.[56]

The incident then took a yet stranger literal turn. Observing the chase, which was now heading south on Amsterdam Avenue, another officer, Patrolman Turner, commandeered a taxi and joined the pursuit. Golden was able to pull within ten feet of the roadster when a shot rang out and he slumped dead over the steering wheel. One of the passengers astutely pulled the car's emergency brake and it stopped, leaving the chase for the moment to Turner. Unbelievably, yet another policeman, Patrolman Klein, jumped into yet another taxi and joined the chase. The roadster went down Amsterdam Avenue to West 63rd Street, then over to West End Avenue and then south to 59th Street, where Morton and a female passenger parked and exited the car. The suspects ran into a cellar, where the two policemen arrested them.[57]

Who fired the shot that killed Golden? It wasn't clear. A .38-caliber lead bullet entering the man's right chest caused his death, said Dr. Thomas A. Gonzalez, acting chief medical examiner. After performing an autopsy, he noted that the bullet had been flattened even though it struck no bones. This was important, as it indicated that the slug might have ricocheted after being fired by Patrolman Ledden (who used a .38). Morton denied having fired from the car, and no gun was found on him or his passenger, in the cellar or anywhere along the crisscrossed route of the pursuit.[58]

A QUARTER-SIZE PIECE OF BLUE CLOTH

In October 1927, there was a tremendous explosion on West 35th Street, completely destroying a tenement building and killing five people and injuring eleven others in it. Gas was known to blow up entire buildings, but this was not the case here. A bomb was responsible for the blast, according to detectives, with one of the five victims the man who was making it at the time.[59]

Police had yet to identify the name of the individual who had been building the bomb, but they were positive it was one of the two "Italian" men who had rented a room for use as a workshop. At first, detectives theorized that the explosion was a vendetta against an Italian barber who owned the building, but an examination of the bomb revealed that it was precisely the same kind that was found a few months earlier in the East River tunnel. Identifying the bomb builder would be difficult if not impossible, as very little of him remained. "The body in the morgue caught the full force of the terrible explosion," a newspaper report stated, with a quarter-size piece of blue cloth the only bit that was left of the suit he had been wearing. Fingerprints were a lost cause; for one thing, his index finger was nowhere to be found. Police believed the two men had been hired to build the bomb, but they had no idea for what purpose it was intended.[60]

SITUATION SERIOUS

The city's homicide squad was probably not happy to learn that they would be working on Christmas Day 1927. But two people were found dead in an apartment on West 46th Street, and questions had to be answered. The first, Peggy Rowan, was a former actress, the second a petty officer whose ship, the USS *Kane*, was currently anchored at the Brooklyn Navy Yard.

Rowan, who was married to another man, had been dead for about five days, seemingly of poison, while L.J. McDaniel, the sailor, about two days. McDaniel was in a room with its door and windows sealed by towels, the gas from a stove still escaping. A letter addressed to a lieutenant was found near his body, and two other notes were discovered. Numerous telegrams were also found in the apartment, all of them sent by to Mrs. Rowan's husband's brother in New York in an attempt to find out what she was up to. One of them ended, "Situation serious."[61]

The following day, police revealed some details about the ugly scene. Rowan had poisoned herself, it appeared, and after a couple of days, McDaniel decided to, in his own words, "go with her." The navy claimed McDaniel's body, while Rowan's husband was on his way from Tampa, Florida, to collect hers.[62]

THE MAYORESS

Greenwich Village was already attracting the bohemian set in the 1920s, and many artistic types and intellectuals knew Amelia Klein, an entertainer in one of the neighborhood's many cafés. Klein went by the name Aimee Cortez and claimed she was twenty-two years old, but her father said she was just nineteen when informed of her death in February 1928. Klein's claim to fame was being recognized as the "Mayoress of Greenwich Village," an unofficial title awarded by the NYU students who lived in the area.[63]

There was no doubt Klein died of gas poisoning in her apartment on University Place, but two very different stories were told regarding the circumstances. The official report was that police, summoned by Klein's neighbors, smashed the door to get in, where they found the young woman dead in her bed. A tube was in her mouth, and the other end was connected to a gas stove, making it a clear case of suicide. A neighbor, however, claimed that it was he who smashed in the door to find Klein in bed after smelling gas. Gas was indeed escaping from the stove, but there was no such tube, leading him and Klein's friends to describe the sad affair as an accident.[64]

Except for a strange incident that had taken place a month earlier, there was little to explain why such a charismatic young woman would take her own life. Klein had won her honorary title as "Mayoress" in a recent election held in the village, having received more votes than another candidate,

A hot dog fair in Greenwich Village, 1917. *Bain News Service, Publisher. Greenwich Village Fair "Hot Dogs," 1917. [June] Photograph. https://www.loc.gov/item/2014704588/.*

Lillian Gusterson. Right after the election, Klein and Gusterson got into a "fracas," causing the former to faint. Gusterson was subsequently found guilty of disorderly conduct, small compensation for her rival's death should it have had anything to do with it.[65]

A RASH DEED

Police suspected murder when they found Leo Murphy dead in the bed of his apartment on East 77th Street in July 1928. His feet were bound and the rope fastened to the bed springs, and around his neck was a noose that had been pulled tight to the head of the bed. The man's nostrils were stuffed with cotton, more evidence to suggest that foul play was involved.[66]

Further investigation revealed, however, that Murphy had killed himself, and in a rather intricate way. The man had been a sailor, the tattoos on his chest, arms and back made clear, making it understandable how he had been able to rig together such a complex system of ropes and knots by himself. A search of his room left little doubt that Murphy was solely responsible for his death. Among his belongings was a letter from a woman warning him of the afterlife consequences of his committing such a "rash deed," and Murphy's own religious leanings were evident on the walls of the apartment. Biblical excerpts such as "Happy is he who trusteth in the Lord" and "Not my will but thine be done" defined the room's décor, suggesting that Murphy had decided to take his chances in the hereafter with his committing the sin of suicide.[67]

YOU CAN'T GO IN THERE

How did Goldie Gross die? The fifty-year-old woman was found dead in her bed in her flat on Essex Street in July 1928, her face covered by a pillow and her nose bruised and bleeding. She had been very much alive just ten minutes earlier, according to a neighbor, adding to the mystery.[68]

Gross and the neighbor had exchanged greetings in the building's hallway, the latter told police, with each woman then returning to her respective apartment on the same floor. Ten minutes later, the neighbor walked over to Gross's apartment to have a chat, but a man blocked her way. "You can't go in there," he said, explaining, "I just came up to see about taking a room here, but Mrs. Gross is busy." The neighbor went back to her apartment but returned a few minutes later, finding the man gone and Gross dead. Did the man, perhaps a robber, kill Gross, or had she had a stroke? Medical Examiner Charles Norris asked himself, hoping an autopsy would answer the question.[69]

THERE HAS BEEN SOME TROUBLE HERE

It was a parent's worst nightmare. The Kohlers' twenty-seven-year-old daughter did not come home one particular evening in March 1929, and Ethel was still missing at 4:00 p.m. the following day. The couple had made repeated phone calls to police but no information as to her whereabouts was forthcoming.[70]

Mr. and Mrs. Oscar Kohler decided to do some investigating themselves. The couple found their daughter's phone and address book and began calling numbers in the hope someone would know something. Someone did. "There has been some trouble here," a policeman answering the phone told Mr. Kohler, "perhaps you had better come here personally." Kohler sped his way to an apartment building on West 76th Street and was admitted by a police officer to a hallway leading to a bathroom. Kohler immediately collapsed. Huddled in the corner was the body of his daughter, dead from bullet wounds in her left eye and chest. The position of Ethel Kohler's body suggested that she had been shot while crouching and likely pleading for her life. Beside her on the floor lay the body of a man, also dead from a bullet through his right temple. He was still clutching a small-caliber automatic pistol in his right hand.[71]

Police were able to put together the pieces of the puzzle. The scene had taken place in thirty-two-year-old Thomas Cronas's apartment, and the man left a note explaining his actions. "She glorified in humiliating me and hurting me," the note read, "and I cannot stand it any longer." Cronas had taken four shots at Ethel Kohler; the two that missed lodged in the bathroom wall. Love letters by the young woman to Cronas were also found in the apartment.[72]

LIFE'S POOR PLAY IS OVER

Having to go through the upcoming trial of two robbers who drove him to bankruptcy was too much for thirty-six-year-old Solomon B. Stein. Four masked men had held up the jewelry manufacturer at gunpoint in October 1928 in his office on West 46th Street, stealing $275,000 worth of precious stones and metals (over $4 million in today's dollars). Stein was questioned at length about the bold theft, the detectives perhaps thinking it may have been an inside job even though the goods were not insured. Nine months later, Stein was subpoenaed by the district attorney to testify against two of the robbers who had been caught.[73]

The mental strain of the ordeal proved excessive for Stein. One night in May 1929, the man went to his office, took off his overcoat, folded it neatly and placed it and his hat on top of a display case. He then wrote a poetic note with a pen, clearly inspired by *Macbeth*. "Tired, he rests, and life's poor play is over," it began, the next line reading, "Approach thy grave like one who draws the draperies of death about him and lies down to dream, and so falls the curtain on the last act of life." Stein then put a tube leading to the gas jet from a furnace in his mouth and lay down on the floor with some cushions propped up around him. Losing consciousness, he grabbed a pencil to scrawl one final non-Shakespearean line. "It takes a lot of gas to kill a man, but it is not so bad."[74]

A DRESSING GOWN AND SLIPPERS

The only thing that seemed clear in the case was that fifty-six-year-old Solomon Bashwitz, who had made much money in the clothing business, was dead from a bullet wound in his apartment in the Hotel Olcott on West 72nd Street. (It was not unusual at the time for wealthy people to live in hotels.) The recently retired Bashwitz had asked his attorney to come to his apartment at 4:00 p.m. one afternoon in June 1929 to meet with him and another lawyer. Bashwitz did not answer telephone calls from his attorney when the latter arrived at the hotel, however, and a bellboy was asked to open the door. Bashwitz, wearing a dressing gown and slippers, was on the floor of his smoking room, the bullet that had pierced his chest and then went through his back now lodged in a bookcase. A .32-caliber automatic pistol lay on the floor near the dead man's right hand.[75]

The scene certainly looked like a suicide, but Bashwitz's attorney and family disagreed. Bashwitz had been murdered, they claimed, citing the absence of a note, no apparent motive and that he did not own the gun as evidence that foul play was involved. An autopsy was ordered by Medical Examiner Norris to confirm his belief that the gunshot was self-inflicted.[76] With the arrest of the manager of Bashwitz's clothing company a couple of weeks later, however, the plot thickened. The manager had allegedly engaged in some financial funny business, according to a district attorney, pocketing $1,125 in a phony sale. Bashwitz had instigated the investigation of the manager before the former retired, it was learned, adding to the theory that he might have been killed. More facts were clearly needed to determine the man's cause of death.[77]

A QUESTION OF MONEY

Jacob Lenart and John Hampl greeted each other cordially when the latter entered the former's speakeasy in August 1929. Hampl had been a friend of Lenart's and sometimes bartended in the little room on the ground floor of a tenement building on East 72nd Street near 1st Avenue. After several drinks together, however, the men's voices began to rise in a heated argument. Suddenly, Hampl drew a .38, causing the seven patrons in the smoke-filled room to scatter, and shot his forty-six-year-old former friend and employer three times through the heart. He then placed the pistol on his temple and fired, completing the murder-suicide.[78]

The loud quarrel was about money, all the drinkers agreed, specifically a certain amount of cash that Hampl claimed Lenart owed him. Arriving at the speakeasy to identify her husband's body, Hampl's wife confirmed that the two deaths revolved around "a question of money." Her husband had been out of work for some time, she told police, not aware that the man was armed when he set out to collect what he believed was due him.[79]

IN A JAM

John Pastorino swore he would not die in the electric chair, and he was good to his word. Hunted by the police for the murder of a tailor (named Versace, oddly enough), Pastorino took matters into his own hands in August 1929. The forty-one-year-old went to the roof of a building on Third Avenue near 49th Street and somehow fired two bullets from his .32-caliber automatic into his head. To ensure he would not be electrocuted for his alleged homicide, he had leaned over the roof when pulling the triggers, as just the fall from the building would likely have resulted in his death. Bloodstains and two empty shells lay near the spot where Pastorino fell, his body striking a hanging sign on its way down to the sidewalk.[80]

Detectives had often heard the man expressing a dread of dying in the electric chair, as well as his vow to commit suicide if he ever got "in a jam."[81]

TAKEN FOR A RIDE

It was likely that many people wanted to see Joseph Chicone, who was considered a "czar" in East Harlem, dead. Chicone a.k.a. Joe Furey ran what was officially called a "private detective agency" that served about two hundred stores and fruit markets between East 100th and 116th Streets. (With its many Italian American residents, the area was known in the early decades of the twentieth century as the "Little Italy" of East Harlem.) Chicone and his staff of twenty-five men "guarded" these retail establishments, in exchange receiving regular payments for the protection. Anyone choosing not to hire his licensed detective agency ran a high risk of something unfortunate happening, however, making such protection essentially a necessary cost of business.[82]

In August 1929, Chicone was found dead in his large and expensive automobile on 1st Avenue near 107th Street, its motor running. Two bullets were in his head, one below the left ear and the other at the base of his skull. The shots had been fired at close range just minutes earlier, evidence that Chicone had been, as police described it, "taken for a ride." Frankie Uale, a Brooklyn gangster who operated his own protection agency, was killed in a similar fashion a year earlier, but that had done nothing to deter Chicone from running his very lucrative business.[83]

THE RACKETEER

A couple of weeks later and six blocks south, another man of dubious character was found dead in an automobile. Like Chicone, Thomas Ahern was a racketeer, but he obtained his dirty money through liquor and drugs. Police didn't know who killed Ahern in September 1929, but they felt confident that it was a competitor who didn't like his recent move into the slot machine business. (James Batto, who specialized in slots, had also been murdered in an automobile within the previous two weeks.) Ahern was a career criminal, having spent his early days in the "Pearl Button" gang, which had its heyday on the Upper West Side about fifteen years earlier. (The nine-member gang got its nickname from the pearl collar buttons on the blue shirts they were known to wear.) Ahern's police record went back to 1909; he had been arrested no less than a dozen times for felonious assault, violation of the Sullivan Act (carrying a concealed weapon), peddling drugs and a variety of other crimes.[84]

While gangsters were bumping themselves off left and right these days, Ahern's slaying was a bit different from the standard mob hit. Usually, the marked man would get a telephone call luring him to a particular spot where his enemies lay in wait and the killing would take place. On his last night alive, however, Ahern walked out of his speakeasy on West 109th Street and then at some point was abducted and taken for his own proverbial ride in an automobile.[85]

THE WEALTHY YOUNG YACHTSMAN

In September 1929, the first of many tragic events to take place at Tudor City—the five-acre faux medieval village on the far east side of midtown Manhattan between 1st and 2nd Avenues and 40th and 43rd Streets—occurred when a twenty-six-year-old man fell or jumped to his death from the Manor. Allen Weir, described as a "wealthy young yachtsman" in a front-page story by a reporter, plunged from his "bachelor apartment" on the eighth floor after drinking late into the evening with two friends. Weir was still breathing when his drinking mates found him on the pavement outside but was not by the time a doctor arrived.[86]

Weir was not just a graduate of the Naval Academy but a brother-in-law of a du Pont heiress, bringing media attention to the case. Detectives interviewed Weir's two friends at length, but the circumstances surrounding the death of the man who dabbled in the stock market when not sailing his yacht *Ceylon* or driving his two expensive automobiles were not all clear.[87]

The Manor in Tudor City. *Historic American Buildings Survey, Creator. Tudor City Complex, The Manor, 333 East Forty-third Street, New York County, NY, 1933. Documentation Compiled After. Photograph. https://www.loc.gov/item/ny1295/.*

A TWO-DOLLAR AND A ONE-DOLLAR BILL

Who would want to kill a seventy-six-year-old invalid widow for three dollars? Detectives from the homicide squad could not immediately say when they found Clara Hewes strangled in her apartment on West 17th Street in October 1929. Just a few hours later, however, they had their man or, in this case, their boy. Twelve-year-old Edward Moran had done the deed, not at all the kind of suspect police usually rounded up for such a heinous crime.[88]

Moran spilled the beans when questioned intensely by police. The boy had been caught stealing three dollars from the woman's moneybox on her bedside table when she awoke from a nap. Hewes, who occasionally told fortunes to visitors, had left her door open, and Moran tiptoed into her bedroom. He was in the act of taking bills from the box, and the woman, upon awakening, told him to put the money back. Moran hesitated and Hewes began grappling with him, but it was no match. The woman had been choked to death.[89]

Moran was quite the criminal in training, throwing a stone through Hewes's transom window after killing her. How did the boy spend the $3.00 that cost a life? Moran played a game of dice with some other boys on West 24th Street, promptly losing $2.50 of it. (He spent the remaining $0.50 on a cake.) An examination of Hewes's bank books revealed that, in hindsight, she should have let the $3.00 go. Hewes had about $15,000 ($226,000 in today's dollars) in savings, making the event that much more unnecessary.[90]

COME TO YOUR MOTHER'S HOUSE

"Come to your mother's house at once," the unsigned November 1929 telegram read, and Esther Schmidt did as she was instructed. The woman arrived at her mother's apartment on First Avenue and, finding the door locked, made her way in through a window reachable from a fire escape. There she found her mother, Eva Hofford, dead from a bullet wound in her left cheek.[91]

Police traced the origin of the telegram to a Western Union office in Brooklyn, and they soon made an arrest near Hofford's residence. Harry Whitman, a night watchman, had sent the telegram, as his handwritten draft had made clear. (Telegram senders would typically write out their messages, which would then be typed by the Western Union clerk.) In Whitman's room were two .38-caliber discharged cartridges, one of which matched the bullet, and the man was charged with murder.[92]

Whitman happened to be deaf, likely the reason why detectives decided to take the man to Hofford's apartment to view the fifty-two-year-old dead woman's body. The detectives wrote out questions for Whitman to answer, but the man was understandably nervous and had difficulty providing any useful information. Further investigation revealed why Whitman did what he did. The man had insisted that Hofford marry him, but she refused, adding insult to injury by getting someone to get Whitman's key to her apartment back. "Never mind, I'll get in anyway," he was heard to say, doing exactly that.[93]

MY DEAR MOTHER

Two women were dead in their room at the Hotel Pennsylvania on 7th Avenue in December 1929, and both detectives and medical officials were admittedly baffled by what had taken place. The bodies lay unclaimed by friends or relatives in the City Morgue, but autopsies would help solve the mystery. The older woman, who had registered as Mrs. Catherine Smith of Boston, died from natural causes, according to Thomas A. Gonzalez, deputy chief medical examiner. Gonzalez was less sure about the younger woman, however, planning to do more tests to learn how and why she died. He did detect that the woman, who had registered as Mrs. M.A. Dreyfus of the same Boston address, had a heart condition, making that a possible cause of death.[94]

Reading a newspaper article about the finding of the two bodies in the hotel, a friend of the women positively identified them at the morgue. Their names were as given, she confirmed, but they lived in Manhattan, adding more mystery to the story. A medical examiner hypothesized that the fifty-year-old Mrs. Dreyfus may have had a heart attack after seeing her mother dead, but only a chemical analysis of her organs would reveal whether she had consumed a poisonous substance. There were signs that that may have been the case. A glass containing a reddish liquid, perhaps mouthwash, was found near the bodies in separate beds, and an unsigned letter from the younger woman to her mother suggested that the former may have committed suicide. "My dear Mother," the letter began, the rest of it expressing her regret that she was unable to spend Christmas with her.[95]

2
THE 1930s

Although the Great Depression came later to New York City than most other places in the United States, Wall Street's laying of an egg in October 1929 altered the trajectory of the city. The numbers of the jobless in Manhattan grew through the early 1930s, and breadlines and panhandlers asking brothers and sisters for a dime became a ubiquitous sight. Fortunately, FDR's New Deal provided much-needed income for the unemployed through his Works Projects Administration, pumping federal dollars into the city's economy.

Alongside this landscape of thrift, paradoxically, was a vibrant entertainment scene in Manhattan. Big bands were literally swinging at hotel ballrooms and nightclubs like the Stork Club, El Morocco, the Cotton Club and the Savoy, with jitterbuggers seemingly unaware there was a Depression going on. High society made their presence known at the Waldorf-Astoria and the Rainbow Room in brand-new Rockefeller Center. Over-the-top movie musicals and madcap comedies were enjoyed by the masses at Radio City Musical on Avenue of the Americas (6th Avenue to real New Yorkers), and the Great American Songbook could be heard played on many a piano all over town.

Some Manhattanites were determined to get rich quickly by taking shortcuts. Until the repeal of Prohibition in 1933, bathtub gin remained a staple of bootleggers who had no qualms eliminating the competition. The 1930s were of course a golden age for organized crime, and gangsters brazenly made hits in broad daylight and took rivals for the proverbial

Berenice Abbott photograph of Rockefeller Center, 1937. *The Miriam and Ira D. Wallach Division of Art, Prints and Photographs: Photography Collection, The New York Public Library. "Rockefeller Center, from 444 Madison Avenue, Manhattan." New York Public Library Digital Collections. Accessed March 27, 2020. http://digitalcollections.nypl.org/items/510d47d9-4f43-a3d9-e040-e00a18064a99.*

Stage at Radio City, 1932. *Gottscho, Samuel H, photographer.* International Music Hall, Radio City, New York. House with curtain down, from main orchestra. *Dec. 7. Photograph. Retrieved from the Library of Congress, www.loc.gov/item/2018734410/.*

ride. This was Mafia Manhattan-style, although there was some crossover with those pursuing similar enterprises in Chicago. In some ways, the island resembled the Wild West, with no shortage of armed bandits on the loose committing robberies and holdups. (They really did say, "Stick 'em up.") Illegal gambling was a popular vice of the era, with a squabble involving the numbers racket leading to someone ending up dead on arrival. Finally, the economic pressures of the Depression led to a fair number of Manhattanites taking their own lives, inscribing the decade with a considerable degree of tragedy.

ALIENATION OF AFFECTIONS

Mrs. Robert Foster, known on the stage as Bobbie Storey, had come a long way in her relatively short twenty-three years. Storey had been named the most beautiful barmaid in Britain in 1923, and the woman left the London public house for New York the following year to play roles in various Broadway productions. Storey had enjoyed considerable success since her arrival but had recently been written out of a show, and no other work was on the horizon.[96]

Hardly a reason to take one's life, especially at such a young age, but that's what Storey did inside the fabulous apartment of an acquaintance on East 38th Street in January 1930. Storey was found dead in the home of F. Raymond Holland, a landscape architect, with gas still escaping from a fire log. The woman's body was clad in a black lace negligee, her purse and a bottle of scotch on a nearby table. "Both purse and bottle were empty," a newspaper article reported, the scene right out of a Hollywood B movie.[97]

It was Holland who discovered his houseguest's body. Having had a nervous breakdown, the man went away for several weeks to recover and was kind enough to allow Storey to stay in his place while he was gone. Holland entered the Moorish duplex on the lower floor and made his way up the winding stairway to the bedroom. A rush of gas greeted him, causing him to shout and, in turn, a French maid to run up the stairs. A physician pronounced Storey dead, with Medical Examiner Norris noting that there were bloodstains on her face and a pillow. Authorities planned to notify the woman's husband in England that his wife was dead.[98]

Not only was Storey married but, as it turned out, so was Holland, who was the son of a prominent Pittsburgh physician. Mrs. Holland had filed a separation suit against her husband, the action no doubt related to another lawsuit she was pursuing. Mrs. Holland was suing one Gladys Watson Ziegler for $300,000 on the basis of "alienation of affections" (an action brought by a spouse against a third party alleged to be responsible for damaging the marriage, most often resulting in divorce). It can be safely assumed that Mr. Holland and Mrs. Ziegler had or were having an affair, making one only wonder what the latter would think upon learning that a dead showgirl had been found in the former's apartment.[99]

A MATTER OF JUSTICE AND HONOR

The police described the unfortunate incident as "an unimportant affair," but Hassan Kadry considered it "a matter of justice and honor." Kadry had shot dead his friend and ex-roommate Kamil Negip. They had come to New York from Constantinople (later named Istanbul, Turkey).[100]

The murder took place in March 1930, but the wheels had been set in motion a little over a year earlier. The two were sharing a flat on Forsythe Street, but Negip decided to move out and asked his friend for a loan of twenty-five dollars. Kadry gave him the money but instantly regretted it when he discovered that Negip had taken the former's spare suit with him. Negip promised he would pay back the money and return the suit but had yet to do so, citing unemployment as the reason for reneging. Kadry had also lost his job, he explained, all the more reason he needed the money and clothes.[101]

Kadry and Negip agreed to discuss the situation at Mehmed Sharif's International Restaurant located on the second floor of a building on Rivington Street. About twenty men sat in the little place, dining, sipping coffee and playing pinochle and 52 (card games). The two quietly discussed the problem until Kadry made a certain remark of which Negip clearly did not approve. Negip walked to another table, picked up a bottle and threw it at Kadry, who, it turned out, was armed. Kadry fired three shots, nearly missing Sharif and a patron who were attempting to grab his gun. Kadry then emptied his pistol, killing Negip, and fled the restaurant. The patrons chased Kadry down the street, the assailant constantly clicking the gun's trigger despite the empty chambers. The men cornered Kadry near a candy stand, but it took a patrolman's billy club to subdue him. "I was robbed and insulted by a man thought to be a friend," Kadry told police at the station house, claiming he had to do what he did out of fairness and respect.[102]

DEATH TAKES A HOLIDAY

In April 1930, Elizabeth Gibbs exited the window of her apartment on the seventeenth floor of Prospect Tower in Tudor City, with the medical examiner ruling it a suicide. The circumstances were both peculiar and newsworthy. The twenty-two-year-old woman was a writer for *The New Yorker*, as was her husband, Wolcott Gibbs (who would go on to achieve considerable success at the magazine).[103]

When questioned, Gibbs told detectives that his wife had been morbidly obsessed with the play *Death Takes a Holiday*, which they had recently seen. His wife had a compulsion to jump from a window since going to the play (whose lead character is Death), he explained, citing that as the reason for her leap. The couple, along with Mr. Gibbs's sister, was actually discussing the

play in the apartment's living room when Mrs. Gibbs calmly and wordlessly walked to the bedroom. After some minutes without her reappearance, Mr. Gibbs decided to investigate and found the bedroom empty. Looking down from the open window, he saw his wife's body on the ground, with a large crowd gathering.[104]

Opposite: Prospect Tower at Tudor City. Historic American Buildings Survey, Creator. *Tudor City Complex, Prospect Tower, 45 Tudor City Place, New York County, NY. 1933. Documentation Compiled After. Photograph. https://www. loc.gov/item/ny1289/.*

Left: Poster for the 1934 Paramount movie *Death Takes a Holiday*, based on the Broadway play.

POSITIVELY IDENTIFIED

Say what you will about the man discovered dead in an automobile on West 213th Street in September 1930, but you'd have to agree that Harry E. Gero was prepared. Not only had the thirty-year-old engineered an elaborate tubing system that flooded the interior of his car with carbon monoxide, but also found nearby were a pound of rat poison and a thick rope long enough to hang a person. His secondary and tertiary contingency plans were not required, however, as the rubber pipe connected to the engine exhaust did the trick. A local resident observed Gero in the rear seat of the running and locked car, assumed he was sleeping and did what he could to try to wake him up. A patrolman was then called, but efforts to revive the man after smashing a window and unlocking a door failed.[105]

If Gero's death was assured by his careful planning, his identity was not. For some time, the man was "positively identified" by police as Edward G. Pennington of Wichita, Kansas, a reasonable conclusion given that Gero had documents on his person bearing that name. A check with police in that state confirmed as much, and the Kansas license plates on his car further convinced New York's finest that Pennington was the methodical dead man. The misidentification ended with a neighborhood canvas and the arrival of Mrs. Gero, however, who told police that she and her husband had arrived in New York just a few weeks earlier.[106]

COWBOY LARRY

Given the number of less than savory characters to be found in lower Manhattan between the world wars, it was quite impressive for "Cowboy Larry" Viscordi to be known as the most villainous man south of 14th Street. But that was the man's claim to fame (or infamy) and a standing that he appeared to fully deserve. Cowboy Larry had once served in the cavalry, hence his nickname, and played up his persona by carrying his pistol like they do in Western movies and shows.[107]

Rather fittingly, then, Viscordi was shot dead late one night in October 1930, his life ending much like that of the town bullies who often populate fictional versions of the nineteenth-century Wild West. Lying beside him at the Black Bottom Club on East Fourth Street was his literal partner in in crime, Charles Grecco. Viscordi was being particularly annoying that evening, throwing lit cigarettes at the members of the orchestra. The four African American musicians dodged the cigarettes and played on, packing up their instruments to go home at 3:00 a.m. Viscordi and Grecco remained seated in the semi-darkened room, apparently having no better place to go, when there was a flurry of bullets. The quartet and three Chinese waiters scampered behind tables and chairs until the firing stopped. Viscordi and Grecco were dead, and one of the band members had been shot but not seriously injured.[108]

Naturally, police had no trouble identifying Cowboy Larry, and Grecco had papers on him that bore his name and address. Viscordi had been shot twice in the head and Grecco no less than nine times. Acting Chief Inspector John J. Sullivan along with some boys in blue arrived on the bloody scene to find the shooter or shooters but, with no definitive answers to what had happened, made no arrests. One theory was that there had been a third party present who left the nightclub and returned with a partner to kill the local gangster and his colleague. Another hypothesis was that the killing was related to Viscardi's tossing of cigarettes at the band. Everyone present agreed that two men were responsible for the shooting and the pair came down the steps leading to the club and fired from the doorway. Any number of people might have wanted Cowboy Larry dead, however, his long list of offenses (which included two homicides) sufficient reason for someone to gun him down.[109]

THE MAN KNEW HOW TO USE A KNIFE

It's impossible to say where John Doe died given that his body's various parts were widely scattered around Manhattan in November 1930. The man's legs, wrapped in sheets, were found in an old suitcase by a street cleaner on an East Houston Street sidewalk near the East River, while his torso and arms were discovered in a trunk fished out of the Hudson River off the West 58th Street pier. The victim's head had yet to be located.[110]

Understandably, given the state of his body, police could not immediately identify the dismembered man. The cause of death was also unknown, as was who was responsible. Detectives had some good clues, however, that could help solve the mystery. Several laundry, cleaning and tailors' marks were found on remnants of clothing in the suitcase and trunk, and a brass claim check was discovered in the pocket of a pair of blue trousers. The claim check was from the Mills Hotel on Bleecker Street, which led detectives to the recovery of a small bag that had been left there. A few articles of clothing were in the bag, as well as an alarm clock and a copy of a Bridgeport, Connecticut newspaper that was a couple of months old.[111]

An autopsy performed by Chief Medical Examiner Charles Norris offered additional information. The victim was a young man, he concluded after the examination, and not a laborer judging by his hands. The man had probably weighed about 145 pounds and was about five feet, eight inches tall (based on his size 16 shirt and size 40 underwear and belt), a physical description that could fit millions of people. What was clear was that whoever had carved up the victim's body was good at his job. "The man knew how to use a knife," Norris remarked, evidence perhaps that the deed was the work of a professional criminal.[112]

A LOT OF NERVE

Two men enter a bar. No, it's not the setup of a joke. Rather, it's what happened in December 1930 in a speakeasy on West 49th Street, when one friend shot another dead after an odd exchange. Forty-two-year-old August Sherman and twenty-nine-year-old Martin Petty were buddies but differed greatly when it came to the ethics of stealing. While they were drinking, Petty took twenty-two dollars from a woman's handbag, leading Sherman to say, "You have a lot of nerve to do a thing like that." A fight started between them, and the proprietor threw them out of the establishment.[113]

The row could and should have ended there, but the brawl continued on the sidewalk until Sherman got into a taxi. Petty followed the cab on foot for a couple of blocks, however, and had his pistol out when Sherman exited the taxi. After firing five shots at Sherman, Petty caught his own cab, but yet another taxi driver who witnessed the attack pursued him. Seeing a patrolman, the cabdriver picked him up, and Petty was soon arrested as he was entering a tenement. Petty's pistol revealed five exploded shells, although he would later tell police that he remembered nothing about the shooting.[114]

A VOLUME OF FRANCIS BACON'S ESSAYS

Nothing in Room 1202 of the Paramount Hotel on West 46th Street seemed right. The guests were not who they claimed to be, for one thing, having registered as Mr. and Mrs. Joseph H. Kane of Scranton, Pennsylvania. The man was actually Joseph H. Zackiewicz of Shenandoah, Pennsylvania, while the woman's identity was unknown. What was clear was that they were dead, the former from a bullet through the head and the latter from two shots just beneath the heart. Zackiewicz still clutched a .25-caliber revolver in his hand, making it appear a murder-suicide.[115]

Detectives were not ready to make such a conclusion, however. No note was left, so the January 1931 case remained open until more evidence was gathered. The mystery woman, believed to be in her late twenties, wore platinum and diamond wedding and engagement rings as well as a silver wristwatch, making robbery an unlikely motive. A traveling bag in the room contained three unopened pint bottles of whiskey and a volume of Francis Bacon's essays, suggesting that at least one liked to drink and read highbrow English literature from the late sixteenth and early seventeenth centuries. Zackiewicz, a former professional football player, had been ill recently, according to his relatives, but they had no idea why he had gone to New York City or who the dead woman in the hotel room was.[116]

DON'T, PAPA, DON'T!

Frances Yitkos of Cherry Street was axed to death in January 1931, but fortunately police had a witness to the ghastly crime. It was a green parrot whose three-word shriek was heard by neighbors in the middle of the night when the murderer repeatedly struck the woman with the hatchet. "Don't, Papa, don't!" the tropical bird was heard to cry when the woman's husband, Frank Yitkos, came after her. The parrot was a notoriously talkative bird but had, to date, limited its chatter to the usual banal banter associated with such creatures. Mr. Yitkos claimed that two men had entered their apartment and attacked his wife when their demands for money were refused.[117]

With the help of the loquacious parrot, however, police arrested Yitkos, although it was unknown whether the bird's testimony would hold up in court if the case went to trial.[118]

A STRANGE CASE

What happened to Angelo Arperidini, a local and well-liked organ grinder? In February 1931, a friend found the man stretched out in bed with his arms tied behind his head and his wrists bound with rope in a Norfolk Street tenement. Death was due to strangulation. One of Arperidini's fortune-telling parakeets was making disturbing noises in the living room, perhaps aware that his or her master was no more.[119]

Detectives could not determine whether Arperidini had somehow committed suicide or was murdered. "It's a strange case," said one of them, suggesting that the man might have been able to thrust his hands through the rope manacles and then extend himself, cutting off his air supply. If it was murder, then who did it and why? Revenge was dismissed as a motive, as Arperidini was a beloved member of the community. A little money was found in the room, suggesting that it was not the work of robbers. Neighbors in the tenement intimated that some believed the organ grinder kept a large amount of cash in his flat, however, the disappointment of not finding such a stash perhaps leading to his death.[120]

YOU GET BACK THERE

It was quite a scene on Chambers Street near City Hall one day in May 1931. Workers in the building were running in all directions, and a large crowd gathered outside it as police sirens screamed. An ambulance from the Beekman Street Hospital pulled up in front of the door and a woman was soon put inside, but the medics could do nothing to help her.[121]

The commotion stemmed from Amy Schuster's refusal to reconcile with her estranged husband, Roy. The couple had been separated for the past five months, and a judge had ordered twenty-six-year-old Roy Schuster to pay his twenty-three-year-old wife forty dollars a week in alimony pending the trial of her suit. Roy had enjoyed success as a vaudeville performer but, as that form of entertainment waned, became a dance instructor, not exactly the best choice of profession in the worst days of the Great Depression. The man then lost that job and, when his marriage failed, made an unsuccessful attempt at suicide.[122]

Things would only get worse for Mr. Schuster. Through her lawyer, Israel Siegel, Amy Schuster filed a motion of contempt of court against her husband when alimony payments were not made. Siegel and his client agreed to meet with Mr. Schuster in the former's office to try to reach a solution out of court, but the young couple, who had been married five years and had a child, was already arguing in a corridor before having their meeting. When Siegel began to escort Mrs. Schuster into his private office, Mr. Schuster attempted to join them, but the lawyer blocked his way into the room. "You get back there," Siegel told Mr. Schuster, but the desperate man had reached his breaking point. Schuster drew a .32-caliber revolver and shot his wife through her head and shoulder, the first one proving to be fatal. As she slumped to the floor, the man fired three more times, with one of the bullets striking Siegel in his arm.[123]

Mayhem then, as the saying goes, ensued. A dozen or so clerks, stenographers and other employees witnessed the shooting, triggering pandemonium inside and soon outside the building. His gun still smoking, Mr. Schuster fled the scene, speeding down two flights of stairs and then taking an elevator to the ground floor. Police were called while Siegel, not seriously hurt, bandaged his arm. Detectives then waited patiently for Mr. Schuster to show up at his home, hoping he would do so rather than make another attempt on his own life.[124]

I'M GOING TO TAKE YOU WITH ME

In July 1931, J. Harry Ballard, a former writer with the *New York World-Telegram*, shot himself in the head in his apartment at the Woodstock Tower in Tudor City. The seventy-nine-year-old man had not recovered from an auto accident he had been in a few years back, something that certainly contributed to his decision to end his life, but there was more to the story. Ballard was forced to retire from his job three months earlier and was given

Woodstock Tower at Tudor City. *Historic American Buildings Survey, Creator. Tudor City Complex, Woodstock Tower, 320 East Forty-second Street, New York County, NY, 1933. Documentation Compiled After. Photograph. https:// www.loc.gov/item/ny1293/.*

a pension, but he clearly missed working at the newspaper, where he had held various positions for the past thirty-three years. He still went into the newspaper's offices every day, eager to help out in any way he could.[125]

Despondent from his physical injuries and his bosses' mandate to no longer write for the paper, however, Ballard had enough. Holding a revolver, he entered his apartment's bathroom and encountered his wife. "I'm going to take you with me," he told her, at which point the seventy-six-year-old woman screamed and fainted. As Mrs. Ballard recovered consciousness, she heard a shot and found her husband collapsed on a sofa in the living room. Neighbors called a doctor, and Ballard was pronounced dead at the scene. The man got the last laugh, however, having written his own obituary and getting one final byline.[126]

SOUNDS OF REVELRY

A wilder night could not be imagined. The September 1931 evening began at a "liquor party" held in the Perry Street apartment of Jack Hartigan, a twenty-four-year-old chauffeur who shared the residence with his brother and mother. Two of the invited guests were twenty-year-old Catherine Cronin and her twenty-four-year-old sister, Blanche, who told their mother they were going to a wedding in Brooklyn. The party was a raucous one, with "sounds of revelry" heard by neighbors in the tenement building until the early hours of the morning.[127]

It would have been a good idea for everyone to have then gone home to sleep it off, but that's not what happened. Led by Hartigan, a group of the revelers, including the two sisters, piled into a taxi owned by a friend of the man, who joined the festivities. Hartigan drove the cab around town, stopping at various speakeasies to keep the party going. Although he drove for a living, Hartigan had partaken of a bit too much revelry and crashed the vehicle into a fire hydrant on Broadway at West 76th Street. The hydrant was knocked off its base, and soon the intersection was flooded with water. Blanche Cronin was thrown into one of the taxi's windows during the crash, giving her a cut on her nose that was soon treated by an ambulance medic. A patrolman arrived on the scene, giving the owner of the taxi (who had slept during the entire joyride), a summons for reckless driving.[128]

Again, that would have been a good time to call it a night (or, in this case, morning), but the worst was yet to come. Hartigan lifted Catherine Cronin

The 1930s

out of the cab, and for unclear reasons, the pair started to walk away. None of the other passengers took much notice of them leaving the scene and could not recall which direction they went. Somehow the pair made it back to Hartigan's apartment, however, where the man's brother woke him up. "Catherine's dead," he told his brother, who sleepily responded, "She was dead when I brought her here." Hartigan had strangled Catherine sometime and somewhere on the way back to his apartment after the taxi crashed, carrying her body upstairs upon arriving at the building. Hartigan then fled from the apartment, and an extensive search for him was soon underway by police when he was not found at his usual haunts.[129]

FIFTEEN FIVE-GALLON CANS

Many a bootlegger met a violent end during Prohibition, but that of Frank Plescia, who also peddled narcotics, was particularly nasty. Plescia was struck with no less than ten bullets when his number was up in September 1931, one of them fired into his jugular vein from close range. A can of alcohol lay beside his body when it was discovered on East 13th Street near 1st Avenue, a fitting thing given the man's trade. The street was crowded at the time Plescia was killed, but true to course, police could find no one who would admit having seen the shooting.[130]

Plescia's murder was likely the result of a feud between like-minded rivals. Much money could be made from bootlegging, so it was not surprising that players in the business often eliminated some competition in such a manner. Regular detainment by police was also just part of the risks associated with the line of work. Plescia, in fact, had been arrested just three weeks earlier, when police found him and a partner driving a sedan with a false bottom concealing fifteen five-gallon cans of alcohol. When his fingerprints were taken for that offense, it was learned that the man had served two terms in the federal penitentiary in Atlanta for the sale of narcotics, but under the name Joseph Meli.[131]

AN ICEPICK OR SHOEMAKER'S AWL

The irony could not be lost when a worker in an undertaker's shop on Monroe Street was murdered in October 1931. The dead man, forty-five-year-old Angelo Lapi, was bound and gagged by a handkerchief and stabbed eleven times in the back and shoulders. His wife, Maria, who worked in the building as a janitor, discovered his body.[132]

Lapi was quite the jack-of-all-trades but, as the saying went, was master of none. For several years, he had worked as a night watchman in his brother-in-law's undertaking place of business, and he made wine and beer that was sold in a nearby speakeasy. Lapi also acted as a collector for what was called the "lottery" or "numbers racket," an illegal form of gambling that was popular among the working class. The man had served two terms in prison, one for felonious assault and the other for violation of the Sullivan Act. Given how Lapi had been murdered, it was likely his part-time gig as a money collector that was responsible. The killer or killers delivered eleven blows with an icepick or shoemaker's awl, according to Deputy Chief Medical Examiner Thomas A. Gonzalez, perhaps by a party who owed a considerable amount of money or had not been paid up.[133]

SILK PAJAMAS

Not one but two "stage girls" were dead in their luxurious apartment in November 1931 at the newly built Parc Vendome on West 56th Street, and there was no dispute regarding the cause of death. Twenty-five-year-old Adelaide Leavy and twenty-year-old Jewel Warner had entered into a suicide compact and lay dead on a mattress in their kitchen. Five burners on the gas range had been turned on and the door and window cracks sealed with clothing and newspapers. They were each wearing silk pajamas.[134]

Why did Leavy and Warner make and follow through with such a pact? A cursory look through the young women's apartment suggested that they did not have money problems. Expensive clothing, many pairs of shoes and even equestrian attire were found in the closets, not exactly the stuff of paupers. Leavy had also written a note leaving jewelry, furs and $1,500 ($25,000 in today's dollars) to her grandmother, making her hardly indigent.[135]

Appearances, however, may have been deceiving. According to their maid, who arrived at the apartment while police were investigating the scene, the women were, in a word, "broke." Warner had told her that they would likely have to dispense with her services, in fact, and a number of people who worked in the building said the two had many unpaid bills and were trying to sell some of their clothing to raise some money. The women were also reportedly out of work, adding to the theory that they took their own lives due to insolvency. Detectives continued to search the apartment, whose walls were covered with framed pictures of motion picture stars of the day, for clues, taking note of the empty quart bottle of whiskey and glass atop the range that had killed them.[136]

MOROSE AND DISCOURAGED

A considerable number of individuals chose to end their lives after losing most or all of their money in the October 1929 stock market crash. Robert Cochran's story was a classic one, symbolizing the emotional downfall many once wealthy people experienced after seeing their fortunes disappear in just a few days.[137]

Cochran had been a successful paint manufacturer, so much so that he was able to invest the $175,000 he reaped from selling his business in the market. The money evaporated with the crash, however, and all the forty-eight-year-old had left was a rooming house on West 71st Street that he rented out to various tenants. By late 1931, Cochran had saved enough money that he could try to recoup some of his loss by speculating once again. Sadly, Cochran lost this money as well, making him "morose and discouraged," according to a newspaper report. He went to the basement of his rooming house and turned on the gas but was found unconscious and survived the suicide attempt.[138]

Cochran's wife kept a close eye on her husband immediately after he returned from Bellevue Hospital, knowing that many people make a second effort if the first one failed. There was no indication that he would do so, however, putting his wife somewhat at ease. In January 1932, just a few weeks after his unsuccessful initial attempt, Cochran arose early, telling his wife that he had to tend to the furnace in the basement. The man had not returned in an hour and a half, however, good reason why his wife went down to the basement to investigate. There she found her husband's body, dead from a bullet fired from a rifle that he had purchased in just the last few days.[139]

I AM ENTIRELY ALONE

An elderly, well-dressed man sat on a bench in Washington Square one sunny morning in February 1932, surrounded by playing children and their nannies. He had strolled down Fifth Avenue and taken a seat near the arch around 10:30 a.m., remaining there for a few minutes. Then he arose, drew a small-caliber pistol from his overcoat pocket, placed the muzzle to his head and fired. A wisp of smoke curled upward from the gun that he still clutched in his hand.[140]

Who was this man, and why did he choose to end his life in such a way? Detectives were on the case, but there were no immediate answers to the questions. In his pockets were a small amount of money, a few pocketknives, a baggage check from the Hotel McAlpin and an unsigned note that read:

> *Will you kindly turn my remains over to a medical college? I am entirely alone. Funds for ambulance charges will be found on my person. Thank you.*[141]

Opposite: WPA photograph of the arch at Washington Square circa late 1930s. *Schomburg Center for Research in Black Culture, Art and Artifacts Division, The New York Public Library. "Rainy Day on the Square" New York Public Library Digital Collections. Accessed March 27, 2020. http://digitalcollections.nypl.org/items/17ca0560-2893-0132-b43b-58d385a7bbd0.*

Above: Hotel McAlpin circa 1910–20. *Detroit Publishing Co., Publisher. Hotel McAlpin, New York City. United States. [Between 1910 and 1920] Photograph. https://www.loc.gov/item/2016812354/.*

A few articles of clothing were found in a bag when detectives presented the baggage check at the hotel. All marks of identification had been removed, however, leaving the man as a John Doe until proven otherwise.[142]

A FERRYBOAT

Police were highly skeptical of what Gerald Greenleaf had written when they searched a room at the Hotel Greystone on West 91st Street in March 1932. His thirty-five-year-old wife, Elsie, lay dead on the bed, the bullet that had been fired from a .32-caliber pistol sitting on a pillow after going through her head. The weapon was nearby on the floor, but Mr. Greenleaf, a former Marine Corps sergeant, was nowhere to be found.[143]

Greenleaf explained what happened in three notes he had left in the room, which they had occupied for the last six months. The man asserted that when he arrived, his wife was trying to strangle herself with a rope, but he was able to stop her. When he went into the bathroom later, however, he heard a shot, and he found her dead. He was so distraught that he left the apartment to commit suicide by leaping from a ferryboat.[144]

Police had good reason to think that Greenleaf's essays were total fiction. Why did he not just shoot himself with the loaded pistol right then and there if he wanted to end his life? Why would the woman try to strangle herself with a rope when she had a loaded pistol (and an extra clip of cartridges)? Where was this rope, anyway? It was not in the apartment, making Greenleaf's story not very believable. The couple owed $114 in back rent to the hotel and another $46 for telephone calls, but Greenleaf had not settled the bill before heading to the alleged ferryboat.[145]

THIRTY PENNIES

Sixty-year-old Estelle Shakleford lived in a dingy room in a tenement on West 59th Street, but that didn't stop a thief from robbing and murdering her in March 1932. Neighbors found the small, frail woman gagged and bound in her bed, the cause of death pronounced by Chief Medical Examiner Norris as asphyxiation. Someone had apparently known that Shakleford, who lived alone and had no friends, had the previous day withdrawn some money from the Franklin Savings Bank at 42nd Street and 8th Avenue. Despite her humble dwelling, she had $1,500, or $28,000 in today's dollars, in her account there.[146]

The $50 Shakleford had withdrawn from the bank was missing from the apartment, although the thief did not bother to take the thirty pennies she kept in a torn piece of cloth tied around her body.[147]

CAPONE'S LIEUTENANT

Police were not immediately sure of the identity of the man who lay beside the dead body of Rosemary Sanborn in an apartment on West 104th Street in August 1932. The man was dead too, having used the same automatic on himself after using it to shoot and kill the woman.[148]

Fingerprint records revealed that the man was Robert Carey a.k.a. Robert Newberry a.k.a. Robert Sanborn, a gangster with deep mob ties. As Robert Newberry, the man had served as a lieutenant for the infamous Al Capone, and police in Detroit were seeking him for the murder of a card sharp named Charles "Doggie" Snyder a.k.a. "The Rat." He was also wanted in Toledo for the murder of a policeman and in Los Angeles for a train robbery. Perhaps his biggest claim to fame, however, was having supplied the police uniforms used by the gunmen in the St. Valentine's Day massacre in Chicago in 1929.[149]

While police across the country were no doubt happy to see Sanborn dead, it was not clear why he had decided to take his life and that of his companion, apparently his wife. A rumor was circulating that Sanborn had kept a list of people he was blackmailing (which included two U.S. senators), but Manhattan borough commander Francis J. Kear denied there was such a list. The Secret Service was investigated the scene, however, as a counterfeiting press was found in Sanborn's apartment, which made it a case for the feds.[150]

A DRUNKEN MAN

Who was the man shot dead on St. Luke's Place in September 1932, and why did his three assailants want him dead? Police believed the twenty-three-year-old man was a chauffeur, his license identifying him as one John Arthur Daggett of the Bronx. But Daggett had not been seen at that address for six months, and no one knew him at an address listed on a previous license. Daggett had been walking east on St. Luke's Place when two shots came from a passing automobile, both of them hitting him in the back. Daggett fell into the street between two parked automobiles.[151]

Police were especially interested in the case because the incident took place just about eighty yards from the residence of former mayor Jimmie Walker, where a patrolman was stationed. There was "a drunken man lying down in the gutter," a small boy told the officer, who had actually heard the shots but thought they were from a car's backfire.[152]

IF I'M FOUND DEAD

Leaving a murder note is highly unusual, but that's what Marian Jennison did at the Cadillac Hotel in Times Square in October 1932. The twenty-five-year-old woman from Milford, New Hampshire, was found dead with a bullet wound behind her right ear. A pistol was clutched in her gloved right hand, however, putting the contents of the letter she had sent to the hotel manager in serious question. "I have everything to live for and no reason for killing myself," Jennison wrote, adding that, "if I'm found dead, you know I have been murdered."[153]

Police were understandably puzzled, unsure if they should believe the evidence at the scene or the note she had written. Things were further complicated when it was learned that a man in an adjoining room came forward to say he had heard a couple arguing in her room and then a shot fired at 3:00 a.m. In her letter, Jennison claimed "a tall dark man" had tried to enter her room, and after scaring him away with her gun, the man told her he "would get me." There was indeed a man in her room that evening, as it turned out, but he told police that no quarrel had taken place. Was Jennison trying to frame the man with a charge of murder? Was she concerned that her family and friends would find suicide a shameful act? The facts remained muddled, but Chief Medical Examiner Norris was sticking to his pronounced cause of death as suicide, as sure as can be that the gunshot was self-inflicted.[154]

AN OIL-STAINED RAG

Medical examiners and detectives typically agreed when it came to stating the circumstances surrounding a person's death. But that wasn't at all the case in October 1932 when William Haskell the Third was found dead in his Park Avenue apartment from a bullet in his head. The basic facts of the incident were plain enough. Haskell, the son of a prominent general (who also happened to be commander of the New York National Guard), was about to hold a dinner party when a shot rang out from a bedroom. Haskell's Japanese butler, Matsui Kamasaka, who had been preparing the dinner, ran to the bedroom to find Haskell shot in the head and dead in a chair.[155]

Upon seeing the body of the twenty-eight-year-old, Dr. Thomas Gonzales, assistant medical examiner, declared it a clear case of suicide, with abundant evidence to support his claim. There was no doubt that Haskell had shot himself, as the man's right hand still clasped a .45-caliber army revolver. Dr. Gonzalez observed that the index finger of Haskell's left hand had a powder burn, a sign that he had used it to steady the muzzle of the pistol against his temple to make sure he wouldn't miss.[156]

John Shields, acting lieutenant of detectives, saw things differently, declaring with equal certainty that Haskell had accidently shot himself. Haskell was thinking about going on a hunting trip, Shields explained, and the gun discharged while the man was cleaning it. An oil-stained rag lay near the chair where Haskell had been sitting, he claimed, making the event a sad mishap.[157]

More information suggested that Shields was likely trying to protect General Haskell from any shame associated with his son's apparent suicide. Haskell III had been a patient in an upstate sanitarium after experiencing "a nervous disorder," the family's physician told police, and there were even newspaper reports of him having suffered a breakdown soon after graduating Princeton four years earlier. Besides all that, why would the younger Haskell elect to clean his gun with an oil-stained rag shortly before hosting a fancy dinner in a Park Avenue apartment? And is an army revolver a good weapon for hunting? Such questions remained unanswered, however, leaving one to make his or her conclusions.[158]

A DOUBLE LOSS

Joseph McReddy and his son, Joseph McReddy Jr., loved Chip, the canary that had brightened up their West 15th Street home with its happy chirping for the past eight years. Mrs. McReddy had died six years earlier, making Chip an even more cherished member of the family.[159]

But now, in October 1932, Chip was dead in its cage, having expired of natural causes. Joseph Jr., a nineteen-year-old student, would be crushed to learn of Chip's demise, Mr. McReddy believed, but luckily his son would not return home from school until later. He would get another canary while his son was out, McReddy told neighbors, perhaps one that looked and sounded so much like Chip that Junior would never notice the difference. He did just that, jubilantly dashing up the stairs to their third-floor flat with a bird that appeared and chirped just like the dearly departed Chip.[160]

While making the swap, however, the new canary flew the coop, darting out an open window. In a panic, McReddy hurriedly made his way up a fire escape leading to the roof to get, well, a bird's-eye view of where the canary might be. The man lost his footing on the second rung of the ladder, which was wet because of a recent rain. McReddy fell to the ground and was now, just like Chip, dead. Young Joseph arrived home a short time later to be told by neighbors of what a newspaper report described as "a double loss."[161]

NONE OF THE DOUGH

A seventy-five-year-old man commits suicide and, in a note, leaves all of his worldly remains to a legatee or heir he named in his final farewell. Happened and still happens all the time. But this time, in November 1932, something was very different. The man's heir was lying dead right next to him, mystifying police from the East 22nd Street station who were called to the scene.[162]

With the air in John Reilly's apartment on East 17th Street reeking with gas and cloth and paper stuffed in the cracks of doors and windows, it was beyond question that the man had took his own life. A note the man left confirmed as much. In it, Reilly designated Otto Lampe of East 19th Street as the recipient of his $132 in the bank and $120 insurance policy (less funeral expenses) as well as all the possessions in his apartment. The problem was that Otto Lampe was just a few feet away, and it was readily apparent that he would never be able to enjoy any of Reilly's bequest. Lampe's brother would be next in line to inherit Reilly's modest legacy, but he was too upset to think about any potential windfall. "I don't want none of the dough," he told a reporter, saying that the death of his brother had "broken me up."[163]

Any number of things could have happened, police reckoned. One theory was that Lampe came to visit Reilly, as he often did, and grief-stricken, decided to join him in the great hereafter. Another was that Lampe was overcome by the gas in the room, making his death an accident, yet another that he had had a lethal heart attack or stroke upon seeing his good friend dead. An autopsy of Lampe's body and the report of the toxicologist represented detectives' best hope to figure out what actually took place.[164]

A GRAND COMEBACK

Larry Fay was a big-time player in Manhattan's Irish mob circles, but by the early 1930s, his best days were well behind him. Fay met his maker on New Year's Day 1933, shot four times by Edward Maloney, a doorman at the Casa Blanca nightclub, on West 56th Street. Maloney's wages, like those of all of the club's employees, had recently been cut by 40 percent, and he decided to take out his frustration on Fay, who had an interest in the Casa Blanca. Witnesses reported Maloney and Fay had engaged in a loud argument immediately before the shots were fired, making the former the prime suspect in the killing.[165]

Newspaper clipping of Larry Fay, 1933. *Billy Rose Theatre Division, The New York Public Library. "Larry Fay. New York Daily Mirror. Jan. 3, 1933" New York Public Library Digital Collections. Accessed March 27, 2020. http://digitalcollections.nypl. org/items/9c53d02f-5526-af99-e040-e00a18061559.*

Mahoney was nowhere to be found, however, and until he was located and his guilt proven, all kinds of rumors circulated along the Great White Way regarding who shot Fay and why. With Fay's long history as a criminal, it was not surprising that many believed that a fellow gangster had eliminated him. Police, meanwhile, were holding the hatcheck girl and four other employees of the club in a midtown hotel as material witnesses. A good number of Fay's friends and associates were sorry to hear the news of his death, but not out of grief. Fay had told those to whom he owed money that he was "on the way to a grand comeback" and had given them postdated checks as a sign of good faith, but now those IOUs were worthless. Fay had exactly thirty cents in his pockets when he was gunned down.[166]

ALIENISTS

In January 1933, the first murder at Tudor City occurred when Evert McCabe, a forty-five-year-old vice president of the United Parcel Service, was shot dead by his wife, Garnett McCabe, on the nineteenth floor of the Woodstock Tower. The story was an especially sad one. Two years earlier, the couple's twenty-two-year-old son had died, reportedly sending Mrs. McCabe into a deep depression. While Mrs. McCabe wanted to constantly talk about their son to keep his memory alive, her husband did not, the reason she gave as to why she shot him in the head at close range at two o'clock in the morning.[167]

The story got even sadder when readers learned that Mrs. McCabe was clutching a picture of her dead soon when police arrived. A suicide note she had written was subsequently found in the apartment. Mrs. McCabe was being held without bail and would be examined by "alienists" (court-appointed psychiatrists who determined the mental competence of defendants) after the case was presented to the grand jury.[168] The woman was committed to the Matteawan State Hospital for the criminally insane and held there for the next three years but was then freed on the basis of her sister's testimony that she had "regained her reason."[169]

LIVING ON FRANKFURTERS

For some unknown reason, the three young men who held up Joseph Arbona in a parked car at 187th Street and Riverside Drive in March 1934 believed they were in for a big payday. The men, all from East Harlem, were behind on their rent, but it was their longing for finer cuisine that led them to commit the heist. "We were sick and tired of living on frankfurters," one of them later told police, apparently thinking Arbona's wallet would be full of cash.[170]

The holdup went "wrong," and Arbona was accidently shot dead, a girlfriend of one of the men reported to the police. Arbona had a total of thirty-six cents in his pockets.[171]

A LONE PROWLER

Who killed William Wy Mon, a wealthy Chinese merchant, in his office on Eldridge Street in October 1934? It was a "lone prowler," according to newspaper reports, but little beyond that could be ascertained. The only witness to the murder was Mon's son, who was just twenty months old and asleep at the time, at least until the three shots from a .38-caliber revolver rang out.[172]

Given Mon's position within the Chinese business community, any number of people might have wanted the forty-two-year-old dead. For close to the past two years, Mon had been president of the Tung On Benevolent Association, whose more than one thousand members essentially ran Chinatown. In addition to heading up that organization, Mon was involved in quite a few business interests. Besides running the Duck Chong Noodle Company and the Far East Chow Mein Company, Mon had a stake in a new snack called Beer Stix, which a journalist described as "a sort of straight pretzel."[173]

Whoever killed Mon in the middle of the night made sure the man would not be alive in the morning. Hearing someone enter his office, Mon turned in his chair, but it was too late. The intruder was pointing a gun at him, and Mon's attempt to shield his face with his hands could not stop a steel-jacketed bullet from striking him beneath his right eye. (The tip of his left pinkie was blown off in the process.) Mon was already dead, his blood-splattered desk littered with fragments of his broken silver-rimmed glasses, but two other shots were then fired into his chest.[174]

Grocery store in Chinatown, 1942. *Collins, Marjory, photographer. New York, New York. Chinese grocery store in Chinatown. New York, United States, 1942. Aug.?. Photograph. https://www.loc.gov/ item/2017835807/.*

Detectives considered the various possible motives for the slaying of William Mon. Like many Chinese, Mon played mahjong but for small stakes, making a gambling dispute unlikely. Robbery too was out, as nothing in his office appeared to have been taken and the man had fifteen dollars in his pocket. Competition in Chinatown had recently intensified, however, suggesting that a business rival could be a potential suspect. Police publicly dismissed the idea that the hit was related to the tong—the Chinese underworld—but members of the community believed it must have been connected to some kind of criminal activity. As the different possibilities were weighed, a large funeral consistent with Mon's high profile was planned.[175]

OKAY, SUGAR

Bonnie Parker and Clyde Barrow had been killed just eight months earlier, but that didn't stop Michael Clancy and Marion Murphy from engaging in a string of robberies that closely resembled those of the famous criminal couple. (Bonnie and Clyde are better remembered for robbing banks, but they actually preferred easier targets like small stores and gas stations.) In just three hours on a single night in January 1935, the twenty-seven-year-old Clancy and seventeen-year-old Murphy robbed four bars and restaurants, killing a man in the process. Clancy had served as one of "toughs" in the Gopher Gang, which operated out of Hell's Kitchen and controlled much of Manhattan's bordellos and illegal gambling.[176]

Clancy and Murphy began their busy night at a restaurant on Columbus Avenue near West 108th Street. At around 2:15 a.m., they took seats in the back and ordered beer, which the proprietor delivered to them. Clancy then ordered him and six customers to the back. "Okay, Sugar," he told his partner, "tap the damper," and Murphy took seventy dollars from the cash register. The couple then sped away in an automobile to the Golf Grill on Amsterdam Avenue, where they followed much the same procedure and netted sixty more dollars. Someone threw a beer mug at them as they exited the place, however, cause for Clancy to shoot and kill forty-five-year-old Michael Cunniff, although it was not clear if it was Cunniff who threw the mug.[177]

Even though they had murdered a man, Clancy and Murphy were not done yet, robbing a café on West 23rd Street about an hour later of forty dollars and, an hour or so after that, a diner on West 33rd Street near Pennsylvania Terminal. Patrons there put up a valiant fight, however, throwing "heavy crockery, cutlery, and sugar bowls," at the couple, as a newspaper reported, which caused them to flee the scene without any money. Clancy's and Murphy's freedom would prove to be short-lived, as the two were arrested that very evening when detectives recognized them in a restaurant.[178]

THAT CRAZY PRIEST

Many understandably wanted to know what took place in a room at the Knights of Columbus Hotel at West 51st Street and 8th Avenue in November 1934. Of the three people in the room that afternoon, only Joseph Steinmetz was alive when he told the story before a jury six months later.[179]

Steinmetz, a twenty-two-year-old former divinity student, had been married just two weeks when a priest, the Reverend Father Joseph Leonard, invited him and his wife to a nearby restaurant and bar. (Steinmetz and his wife were staying in one room in the hotel, and the priest in another.) Steinmetz was not a big drinker but complied with the priest's urging to have a few cocktails. "That crazy priest took us to a restaurant at 48th Street and made us drunk," he stated in court, adding that he had had "four highballs." Leonard then reportedly pressed Steinmetz to drink some more while the priest and the man's wife returned to the hotel. After a short while, Steinmetz returned to the hotel and went to the priest's room, where he found his wife and Leonard partly undressed and kissing.[180]

Steinmetz happened to be carrying a loaded revolver and shot them both. "You kissed each other and you're going to heaven," he recalled he told them before firing the gun four times. Steinmetz believed it had been the priest's intention to get his wife drunk in the hope he could have sex with her, something the jury might consider as they determined his fate.[181]

A CONSTANT POUNDING IN MY HEAD

Harry Confess wanted to kill someone, so he decided to kill himself instead.[182] In May 1935, the forty-five-year-old man who ran a gift shop in Atlantic City, New Jersey, checked into the Hotel Edison on West 47th Street and shot himself. The aptly named Confess explained it all in a note he left. "For sixteen months I've fought the obsession to kill," he wrote, blaming an unnamed man for causing a friend's wife to kill herself. "There's a constant pounding in my head," he continued, saying that if he did not kill that man or himself, "I'll go insane." Confess chose the latter.[183]

TWO RICKETY CHAIRS

When her husband had not returned home by 11:00 p.m. one evening in December 1934, Jenny Silverstein called the police. The next morning, Max Silverstein had been missing twenty-four hours, the required amount of time to launch an investigation. Detectives soon learned that Silverstein, a salesman for a jewelry firm, had received a call from a man who said he was interested in buying some unset diamonds. The man asked Silverstein to meet him at his office on Canal Street, and as instructed, the forty-year-old salesman went to Room 605 of the appointed address. He was carrying $6,000 worth of gems. Silverstein had previously made sales calls in that very building, so nothing seemed suspicious.[184]

Detectives proceeded to Room 605 of the Canal Street building whose door was inscribed "Stern & Weiner, Jewelry Setters." The door was locked, and no one answered the two detectives' knocking, leading them to peek through the keyhole. The body of a man lay on the floor, and after being let in the office by the superintendent, it was clear that they had found the missing Silverstein. His hands and feet were bound with copper wire, and a handkerchief was stuffed into his mouth. He had also been struck in the head, although it was not immediately clear whether that was the cause of death or if he had suffocated. Beside his body was the case in which he had carried the diamonds, now empty.[185]

Where were Stern and Weiner, and why was their office entirely empty save for "two rickety chairs"? The so-called jewelry setters did not exist, of course, the operation a complete setup. A man, no doubt using an assumed name, had rented the office about ten days earlier, the superintendent told the detectives, putting thirty-five dollars down as an advance on the rent. This was the third such robbery of jewelry salesmen in the building within the last few weeks, it was later learned, something Silverstein had obviously not known.[186]

THE CHINESE EASTERN RAILWAY

Who owned the Chinese Eastern Railway in Manchukuo in 1934? Not something to shoot someone over, most would agree, but that's what happened on a West 23rd Street ferry slip in December of that year. For more than a year, two peddlers, one Russian and one Greek, argued over which country possessed the rights to the railway in northeastern China. John Lazos, the Greek, sold hot dogs and lemonade from his cart near the Central Railroad of New Jersey ferry house, while Kagen Der Tarvanian, the Russian, peddled oranges and pears from a box on 12th Avenue near 22nd Street, which was close to that ferry house. The fact that both men operated their respective business near the railroad ferry house likely accounted for their mutual and passionate interest in railways, even though the one in question was located on the other side of the world.[187]

Building the Chinese Eastern Railway, 1908–1913. *Education Association, Moscow, Creator. Vid" na vremiãńku i liniiũ u kosogora versty 19-ĭ. Reĭnovskaiã̂ vĭeĭv'. Nanagry Russian Federation Zabaykalsky Krai, 1908. Moscow, Russia, to 1913. Photograph. https://www.loc.gov/item/2018682960/.*

One day Der Tarvanian, who almost certainly argued that the railway was owned by the Russians (versus the two other possibilities, the Chinese or Japanese), had enough. He drew his Colt .32 automatic and shot Lazos twice, one in the spine and one in his left arm. Two patrolmen who happened to be in the area and heard the shots ran to the scene, where they were met by additional firing from Der Tarvanian. The shots went wild (one ricocheted and hit a taxicab driver in his foot), but the Russian hid behind a truck and reloaded his pistol. The patrolmen pursued Der Tarvanian into the ferry house, where the man fired all six shots, these too going astray. (Der Tarvanian had not even held the gun in seven years, he later told police, having taken it out specially that day to shoot his fellow peddler should he bring up the subject of railroad ownership.) Der Tarvanian then hurled the gun at one of the cops, who fired a bullet into his right calf. The Russian was able to hobble to the baggage room, where he was subdued. Lazos died an hour and a half later from his injuries at St. Vincent's Hospital, and Der

St. Vincent's Hospital, 1933. *Historic American Buildings Survey, Creator, Education And Welfare Department Of Health, and Robert S Lange, Zane, Steve, photographer. St. Vincent's Hospital Complex, 153 West Eleventh Street, New York County, NY, 1933. Documentation Compiled After. Photograph. https://www.loc.gov/item/ny0424/.*

Tarvanian was arraigned for homicide. For whatever it was worth, the latter was correct: at that time, the Russians owned the rights to the railroad (but would sell them just a few months later to the newly established Manchukuo government.)[188]

PEOPLE WERE FOLLOWING ME

It certainly wasn't a good day for Saverio Bongiorno or the man he killed, James Gerrity. The episode that took place at the Hotel Edison on West 47th Street in January 1935 was a particularly strange one. Bongiorno, a fifty-nine-year-old real estate and insurance broker, had registered at the hotel with a small beach bag as his only baggage (despite having no permanent home). At 9:00 p.m., he called the switchboard operator and asked that a physician be called to his room. Hotel management sent a bellboy to Room 1135 to investigate the situation, but Bongiorno did not answer repeated knocks. The guest then called the operator two additional times making the same request, but Bongiorno again did not open the door for the bellboy.[189]

Management decided to try a different tack, asking Gerrity, the chief house detective, to go up to the room to find out what was going on. (Gerrity was just finishing dinner with police lieutenant James Finn, whose claim to fame was having arrested Bruno Richard Hauptmann, who was convicted of the abduction and murder of the Lindbergh baby.) Like the bellboy, Gerrity knocked on the door repeatedly but, with no answer, decided to use his passkey to enter the room. As he inserted his key, the door swung open and there was Bongiorno, a .38-caliber pistol in his hand. Gerrity turned to flee, but Bongiorno fired twice, one of the shots hitting the detective in the base of his skull. While other guests on the floor frantically called the switchboard after hearing the shots (and perhaps opening their doors to see the dead detective), Bongiorno calmly asked the operator to be connected with police headquarters. Bongiorno surrendered quietly to the police and confessed to the crime at the station. He had no motive for the shooting, he explained, simply saying that "people were following me."[190]

BY THE TIME YOU RECEIVE THIS

One day in April 1935, Charles Biermann mailed a letter to his brother Louis even though the two were going to have dinner and see a movie that night. The brothers did indeed spend the evening together, with Louis saying later that Charles seemed unusually cheerful given the latter's recent despondency. When they departed, the men agreed to go to a baseball game sometime soon.[191]

Hotel Piccadilly. *Irma and Paul Milstein Division of United States History, Local History and Genealogy, The New York Public Library. "227 West 45th Street (Seventh Avenue–Eighth Avenue)" New York Public Library Digital Collections. Accessed March 27, 2020. http://digitalcollections.nypl.org/items/510d47e2-c352-a3d9-e040-e00a18064a99.*

Louis was thus quite surprised to receive a letter the following day from his brother. "By the time you receive this I will be dead," the letter began, spurring Louis to race to the Hotel Piccadilly on West 45th Street, where Charles was living. With the house detective in tow, Louis entered the room and found his brother on the floor dead. A towel lay across his face, and on a nearby table was an empty glass, which was soon determined to have contained a poisonous liquid. Two other suicide notes, also addressed to relatives, were found in the room.[192]

As a real estate dealer, Charles Biermann had prospered, his brother told detectives, but the Depression put an end to the good times. He'd lost $250,000 in the past five years and was nearly out of money, Louis explained, the reason why his brother had in the past raised the subject of committing suicide. Louis thought Charles might have put such thoughts out of his mind after spending the happy evening with him, but it was not to be.[193]

LITTLE THINGS LIKE THIS

One of Dick Butler's sons was dead as a result of a gang war in March 1936, and the man was sure the newspapers had got which one it was wrong. "No, that can't be right," Butler, a former Tammany Hall assemblyman who had run the west side docks for twenty years, said, thinking it had to be Joe rather than the reported Richard. Butler called a couple of undertakers, but they didn't know, so he headed to the West 30th Street police station to

Hotel New Yorker, 1930. *Irma and Paul Milstein Division of United States History, Local History and Genealogy, The New York Public Library. "481 Eighth Avenue (34th Street–35th Street)" New York Public Library Digital Collections. Accessed March 27, 2020. http://digitalcollections. nypl.org/items/510d47e2-f250-a3d9-e040-e00a18064a99.*

learn the truth. Just as he thought, it was indeed Joe, detectives told Butler, the hit related to some kind of labor trouble on the docks or ownership of goods that had been hijacked from a truck.[194]

While the specifics were not yet known, it was clear that Joe Butler had been gunned down near the Hotel New Yorker on West 34th Street. He along with two others had been walking to a parking lot when a car approached them. The muzzles of two sawed-off shotguns poked through the windows, and gunfire reverberated down the street. Joe Butler was hit in the abdomen and face and died soon after the shooting. Whatever he was involved with, it was highly likely that it was illegal, as the man's criminal record listed eleven arrests (but just three convictions). Although just four of his ten children remained alive, Dick Butler did not seem particularly fazed by his son's violent end. "Little things like this happen in any family," he told a reporter, taking consolation in the fact that it would have been impossible for him to have prevented it.[195]

A SMALL RIOT

Mayor Fiorello LaGuardia was looking forward to the concert being held at Lewisohn Stadium, an amphitheater on the campus of the City College of New York, one evening in July 1936. While on the way to the stadium in his chauffeur-driven car, however, a police call came on the radio, instructing officers in the area to proceed to 7th Avenue and West 116th Street. His reputation as a man of action was well deserved. LaGuardia told his driver to divert to the scene, as it was just a few blocks away. A man (described by a reporter as a "Puerto Rican Negro") had been shot and killed, and soon more than one hundred policemen arrived at the intersection to maintain order.[196]

The police and the mayor had good reason to be concerned about crowd control after such an event. For the past six months or so, the area had

Mayor Fiorello LaGuardia at his desk, 1939–40. *Manuscripts and Archives Division, The New York Public Library.* "LaGuardia, Fiorello, H.–Signing Holiday of Joy Proclamation" *New York Public Library Digital Collections. Accessed March 27, 2020. http://digitalcollections.nypl. org/items/5e66b3e8-79b5-d471-e040- e00a180654d7.*

been the site of major street disorder related to Italy's recent invasion of Ethiopia. Twenty extra policemen had been stationed in the neighborhood, where considerable numbers of both African Americans and Italian Americans lived. A few days prior to the shooting, ten more cops were added to the area after there was a confrontational demonstration in which three policemen were injured. Stones were thrown through the window of a restaurant owned by an Italian American, triggering what was termed "a small riot."[197]

The shooting acted as a lightning rod in the already tension-filled neighborhood. Soon more than one thousand people were milling about, with Mayor LaGuardia right in the middle of it all. Many more peered out from windows, rooftops and fire escapes, wondering who had shot whom and why. Bernel Saunders, a thirty-three-year-old African American former boxer, had repeatedly shot thirty-six-year-old Raymond Lopez after the two exchanged words in front of a flower shop, although it was not clear if the dispute had anything to do with international politics. The mayor congratulated nearby policemen for keeping the situation in hand and attempted to return to his car. That was easier said than done, however, as his way was blocked by hundreds of people, most of whom did not recognize him (or perhaps did not notice him, given that the man stood five feet, two inches tall). LaGuardia's decision to disrupt his plans for the evening and place himself in a potentially dangerous situation (he was Italian American, after all) was rather remarkable, but in true fashion, "The Little Flower" said it was nothing.[198]

WELCHED ON A BET

Dominic Didato probably knew what awaited him when he was ordered by a foe to exit a restaurant on Elizabeth Street in August 1936. The assailant fired four bullets into Didato and fled the scene, just another unsolved gangland slaying.[199]

Given his résumé, Didato's murder was not at all surprising. The thirty-nine-year-old native of the Lower East Side had been a childhood buddy of Salvatore Lucania a.k.a. Charles "Lucky" Luciano, and the two spent much of their respective careers together as adults. Didato went with Lucania when the latter decided to join forces with the Chicago-based Al Capone. Lucania's luck ran out several years earlier, however, and he was now serving thirty to fifty years at Dannemora prison for compulsory prostitution. Didato tried to take over Lucania's operations but failed, and he was keeping busy as a small-time bookmaker. Didato had "welched on a bet," police believed, leading to his death just a few blocks from where he grew up.[200]

ACCIDENTALLY STUMBLED

William Noyes certainly had seen better days. The fifty-six-year-old had graduated from Princeton and served as a lieutenant during the Great War before becoming an executive with the Equitable Trust Company. By June 1937, however, the ex-banker had fallen on hard times, living in a small room in the basement of a building on West 89th Street and reportedly depending on small gifts of money from college classmates to survive.[201]

Given his descent, one might understand why Noyes was asleep in his bed one afternoon, a bottle of whiskey beside him. Mary Hunter, Noyes's common-law wife, however, apparently had little sympathy for the man's plight. She grabbed for the bottle, and a struggle ensued. Hunter picked up a paring knife, into which Noyes "accidentally stumbled," as she later told detectives. Noyes was dead, the four-inch blade still sticking out of his left chest.[202]

Detectives grilled Hunter for hours, but the woman continued to insist that she had not intentionally stabbed Noyes. A pair of assistant district attorneys then led another extensive round of questioning, with Hunter not changing her story. The DAs were not buying what Hunter was selling, however, and the woman was booked on a charge of homicide.[203]

FAIRLY WELL DRESSED

It was unusual for a twenty-eighty-year-old man to die of some natural cause, but that was what a doctor from Columbus Hospital pronounced after examining the body of Louis Amorelli in July 1937. A passerby had found the man lying on an Elizabeth Street sidewalk at 1:40 a.m., but the physician saw no reason to believe Amorelli had had some kind of accident or met a violent death.[204]

It was only when Amorelli's clothing was searched for identification at the station house that it became clear how the man actually died. Four bullets were in Amorelli's back, something the doctor had somehow not noticed. Positive identification by fingerprints made it not too surprising that the man had been shot and killed. Eight years earlier, Amorelli had been arrested after holding up a radio shop, and he had spent most of that time in Sing Sing. Police were trying to figure out what Amorelli had been up to since getting

Sing Sing prison, 1938. *Stieglitz, C. M, photographer. Old cell block, Sing Sing Prison where Richard Whitney is housed / World Telegram photo by C.M. Stieglitz. New York Ossining, 1938. Photograph. https://www.loc.gov/item/98500204/.*

out of prison eight months earlier in order to solve the murder. Whatever it was, Amorelli seemed to have been doing quite well given the fact that he was, according to police, "fairly well dressed."[205]

YOUR HONOR, HE'S DEAD

Relatives and colleagues of Robert Gray were present in Felony Court one morning in August 1937, hoping their support could help get the charges that had been made against him dismissed. The fifty-five-year-old man had been accused of stealing $25,000 by forging the name of the head of his company on some fifty checks. After cashing those checks, he fiddled with the books to cover his tracks, so there appeared to be sufficient evidence to find him guilty. Gray had earlier pleaded not guilty to the charge, but he admitted to the judge that he had a taste for luxurious things, something that no doubt did not help his case.[206]

When Magistrate Andrews called out Gray's name to appear before him in court, however, it was a detective who came forth. "Your Honor, he's dead," the detective announced, explaining to the judge that Gray had hanged himself in his cell in the "Tombs" (City Prison) on Centre Street about three hours earlier. Gray had made a noose out of his belt and tied it to a bedsheet, choosing death over a possible long prison sentence.[207]

HAVING A WONDERFUL TIME

The audience at the Lyceum Theatre on West 46th Street right off Broadway was likely having a wonderful time at the show they were attending in November 1937, coincidentally called *Having a Wonderful Time*. In his office on the second floor, however, Spencer Bettelheim, a theatrical executive, was suffering greatly, and not because of a poor box office. Rather, Bettelheim was in "agonizing pain," as he described it, having terrible headaches that he could not soothe.[208]

Bettelheim knew exactly why he was in such dire physical straits. Twenty years or so earlier, Bettelheim was in France serving with the 306th Infantry, 77th Division. In 1918, his division engaged in the Battle of the Meuse-Argonne, in which Germans used mustard gas on the Allied forces. Like

The Tombs, or City Jail, in 1905. This building stood until 1941, when the Manhattan House of Detention was opened. *Detroit Publishing Co., Copyright Claimant, and Publisher Detroit Publishing Co. The Tombs, New York. United States, ca. 1905. Photograph. https://www.loc.gov/item/2016799915/.*

many who were exposed to the gas, Bettelheim had never been the same, his body unable to fully repair itself. In 1932, the city of Verdun, France, awarded him a citation and medal in recognition of his service at that battle, but it did nothing to stop his unbearable pain.[209]

Although Bettelheim was just forty-three years old and had a successful career and family, he'd had enough. The man shot himself in the head with two bullets likely while his show was being enjoyed in the theater just steps away from his office. Bettelheim had planned to attend a prizefight at the Hippodrome with his nephew, and it was he who found his uncle's body at 11:30 p.m. when the man didn't show.[210]

SEVEN DOLLARS A WEEK

The death of Claude Kendall was worthy of one of the mystery novels he used to publish. In November 1937, Kendall was found dead in a seven-dollar-a-week room of the Madison Hotel on East 27th Street, a bedsheet wrapped around his neck.[211]

Detectives could not figure out what had happened in the room. The forty-six-year-old ex-publishing executive had not been robbed, they concluded, nor had there been a struggle in the room. Medical Examiner Thomas Gonzales did observe that Kendall had a black eye, a cut on his lip and a swollen jaw, however, indications that something of a violent nature had occurred. Interviews revealed Kendall had been drinking the prior evening, so much in fact that he had to be taken to his room by two friends. Kendall had no injuries when they put him to bed, they made clear, adding that they left him dressed but did take off his shoes.[212]

When the maid found Kendall's body the following morning, however, the man had his shoes on. A tenant on the floor above said he heard some thumping at 4:30 a.m., leading detectives to think that Kendall might have received his injuries by bumping into the furniture. The case remained a mystery, a fitting end for a man who had been in the whodunit business.[213]

TWO KITTENS

It was probably while drinking most of a quart of liquor that things between forty-five-year-old William King and thirty-five-year-old Harriett Nielson got out of hand in February 1938. The two had met around 4:30 one afternoon and then went to dinner, where Nielson, who was married to someone else, had several drinks. The couple bought a pint of gin on the way to the woman's home on West 76th Street, with Nielson consuming most of that, which is when they purchased the quart of liquor.[214]

With that much alcohol drunk in a single evening, it wasn't surprising that the date got a bit crazy. At some point, Nielson, who came from a well-to-do California family and had been an Olympic swimmer, accused King, a WPA musician, of chasing her two kittens out of her apartment. A quarrel ensued, leading to Nielson hitting King in the face with the empty gin bottle. His face cut, King retaliated by slapping Nielson, which is where his story began to get somewhat fuzzy. Nielson fell several times, but he picked her up each time, King claimed, after which he went to sleep. When he awoke, Nielson was dead on the floor, her death perhaps the result of a fall. Detectives were skeptical of King's version of the evening's events, however, and booked the man for homicide.[215]

THE HATCHECK GIRL

Did Norma de Marco jump from her friend's apartment on West 58th Street in April 1938? Or was she pushed out the window of the building? Either way, her death no doubt stemmed from a holdup of the Howdy Club in Greenwich Village that had taken place a few days earlier. During the heist, in which twenty-five customers and employees were robbed, de Marco was struck on the head with a gun by one of the crooks. Police engaged in a gun battle with the three robbers, and soon two of them and one patrolman were wounded. The twenty-eight-year-old, who was a hatcheck girl in another club, had moved into her friend's flat since the robbery and, as a witness to the crime, been questioned by the District Attorney just the day before her death.[216]

Why had de Marco moved out of her own apartment? Was her life in danger because of her being a witness? Most important, who were the two men who were observed visiting her friend's apartment the very evening that she leapt or was murdered? A cop had been shot in the head and was in serious condition at Bellevue, all the more reason why detectives were asking these questions and were determined to learn the answers.[217]

CLOSE TO THE ONE I LOVE

Seth Avery was free on bail in April 1938, but he clearly did not want his case to go to trial. He and three other men were accused of extorting $21,000 from a retired schoolteacher over the past year by posing as Internal Revenue Service agents. The men apparently coerced the woman to pay them the taxes she likely did not owe, and it was a crime to impersonate a federal agent. Avery had posted $10,000 in bail money but decided to kill himself by gas in his apartment on Lexington Avenue near East 34th Street.[218]

While his ethics may have been questionable, Avery was a proud member of the American Legion (United Manhattan Post 9), and he chose to wear his uniform when he opened the jets of the gas range in his kitchen and put a connecting rubber tube in his mouth. A note confirmed that it was no accident. Avery wrote that he wanted to be buried "close to the one I love," although it was not clear who that was given that the man was separated from his wife.[219]

DON'T LIGHT MATCHES

Neel Enslen had a great voice. While in Chicago, the man was an original member of the American Opera Company, and he came to New York in 1929 when radio was all the rage. Without any training in radio whatsoever, Enslen auditioned for an announcing job and, against all odds, got it, reportedly the first time that had happened in the industry.[220]

In May 1938, Enslen was a radio announcer for NBC, but the forty-five-year-old baritone was seriously ill. He took a two-week vacation to rest up, but the night before he was supposed to go back to work, he decided to take his life instead. While his wife was visiting some friends, Enslen posted a sign near the front door of his apartment on Haven Avenue that read, "Don't smoke cigarettes, don't light matches." Then he opened five jets on the gas stove in the kitchen, the reason why he thoughtfully cautioned anyone who might find his body.[221]

FORTY MINUTES

The city marshal was on the way one day in May 1938. Frank Bryson had done everything he could to pay his rent. The sixty-year-old man had sold newspapers and rented out rooms in the seven-room apartment on West 83rd Street, but it wasn't enough. In less than an hour, the marshal would put him and all his belongings on the sidewalk, a dismal prospect given that Bryson had nowhere to go and no money to rent another place.[222]

With forty minutes to go before the eviction, Bryson picked up his .38-caliber pistol and put a bullet in his right temple. The man, who had once been the proprietor of a poolroom on Broadway, left five notes to friends and relatives, explaining to each of them why he did what he did.[223]

I WILL MEET YOU IN THE NEXT WORLD

Irene Racz had an impressive career since arriving in New York in 1930. The thirty-year-old Hungarian artist had had her work shown in a number of Manhattan galleries, with critics noting the decorative quality of her paintings. But Racz decided to end her life in August 1938, taking an excessive amount of a "sleeping potion" in the suite she shared with her mother and a dog at the Hotel Oliver Cromwell on West 72nd Street. Racz did not provide a motive for her action, but she did leave a note to her mother in her native language. "I am going to commit suicide and I want you to give the dog some of the poison and take the rest yourself," she wrote in Hungarian, adding, "I will meet you in the next world."[224]

Racz's mother, however, was not at all ready to go to the next world. Rather than kill herself (and the dog), the woman called the hotel's management for help, but it was too late for her daughter, who would have to wait to meet her mother again.[225]

A MAN'S CRY FOR HELP

Quite mysterious were the circumstances surrounding the tragic end of a married couple in September 1938. Raemer Renshaw, a fifty-eight-year-old professor of chemistry at NYU, and his wife each fell to their deaths from the nineteenth floor of Prospect Tower of Tudor City, with police having no idea what had previously transpired inside their apartment. Renshaw left his office around 5:00 p.m. in good spirits, colleagues told police, but he apparently did not return home until 11:00 p.m. A number of neighbors heard a man's cry for help about that time and began to call the building manager on the house phone, but it was too late. The two bodies soon hit the ground, with few clues to determine the course of events that had led to their deaths.[226]

A search of the Renshaws' apartment did suggest that Mrs. Renshaw was in bed when her husband arrived home. The professor's coat and hat were hanging on a chair, suggesting he had no plans of leaving the apartment that evening, and there were no suicide notes found. All kinds of theories were in play as police tried to reconstruct the facts.[227]

BRILLIANT, EMOTIONAL AND HIGHLY SENSITIVE

Why would two twenty-three-year-olds with so much to live for forge a suicide pact? Police had theories when they found the bodies of the married couple in their apartment on East 97th Street, but there were still many questions to have answered. Sonja Lewis, a German refugee, and her husband, Hudson Lewis, were dead from gas poisoning in December 1938, with the contents of four notes left by the couple not providing a definitive reason for their decision. The couple had a three-year-old child who was sent to Sonja's parents while the event took place.[228]

Described by friends as "brilliant, emotional and highly sensitive," the Lewises had an interesting history. In 1934, Sonja fled from Germany to England, where Hudson was living, to escape rising anti-Semitism. The couple had recently immigrated to America, and their future looked bright despite having little money. Sonja aspired to be a writer, while Hudson was an expert in international affairs. It wasn't unusual for people that age, especially those new to the country, to struggle financially, and police believed that could have been why they took their lives together.[229]

Another, odder theory was in play, however. Friends believed it was not a lack of money but some recent news that drove them to open the five gas jets on their range. Sonja Lewis had just learned that her grandmother in Frankfort, Germany, died from shock after Nazis destroyed the Jewish home for the aged where she lived. While certainly a terrible thing to have happened, would it drive a young couple with a child to suicide? No one could say for sure, leaving the case as a mystery.[230]

THROW UP YOUR HANDS

Robberies always tended to spike in the days leading up to Christmas, and 1938 was no exception. Jewelry stores and rare coin dealers were at particular risk because their goods were both valuable and portable. Edmund May, assistant manager of Rud Kohler, a rare coin dealer on Fifth Avenue, was fully aware of the risks involved with keeping his shop open the day before Christmas Eve. But May was well prepared for any eventuality, and not just because it was the holidays. Four years earlier, in the very same office, three holdup men had badly beaten up the founder of the firm, Rudolph Kohler, during a robbery, and Kohler had subsequently died of his injuries.[231]

Although May was not in the store that day, he worked for Kohler at the time (and was related to him), and he was determined that history would not repeat itself. In walked Albert Weiner, a career criminal who had been arrested an average of one time a year for the past eighteen years, along with a neatly dressed companion. "Throw up your hands," Weiner, who was armed with a pearl-handled .32-caliber revolver, told May. May whirled and dashed through a door leading to the back room. Weiner fired but missed, and May returned to the showroom, holding his own, more deadly weapon. May fired his .45 repeatedly at Weiner and the well-dressed man, hitting Weiner once in the left side and once in the head. Weiner was down, and May emptied his gun at the other, fleeing man. The dapper man escaped, but Weiner would soon die from his pair of bullet wounds.[232]

WHEN IS AN AMBULANCE COMING?

Early one morning in September 1939, Joseph "Little Joe" La Cava and Rocco "Chickie" Fago lay under a pile of broken bottles and smashed chairs and tables outside the O Sole Mio Café on Mulberry Street. Nothing could be done for the forty-year-old La Cava, as he was dead from a bullet wound in his left temple. Fago, also forty, was still alive, however, propped up against a soft drink stand on the sidewalk. "When is an ambulance coming?" Fago moaned, in considerable pain after having been shot in the shoulder.[233]

The facts surrounding such cases are often unclear, but in this one, police knew precisely why the two men had been shot. La Cava and Fago were part of a ten-member racket union that shook down small café owners in the neighborhood for "protection." The two men, who were

Berenice Abbott photograph of Mulberry Street at Prince Street, 1935. *The Miriam and Ira D. Wallach Division of Art, Prints and Photographs: Photography Collection, The New York Public Library. "Mulberry and Prince Streets, Manhattan." New York Public Library Digital Collections. Accessed March 27, 2020. http://digitalcollections.nypl.org/items/510d47d9-4fbe-a3d9-e040-e00a18064a99.*

close friends and ex-convicts, had been recently indicted by a grand jury on that charge but were free on bail. La Cava and Fago had spent the prior evening demanding fees from café owners for their supposed service, mixing business with the pleasure to be had during the weeklong San Gennaro festival that the neighborhood was famous for. One café owner, perhaps that of O Sole Mio, had turned down the pair's offer and in an obviously demonstrable way.[234]

As usual, nobody in the area reported having witnessed any kind of disturbance inside or outside the café, leaving detectives with the task of finding out exactly who had declined the men's proposal.[235]

TO JOSEPH

Ten families were living at 181 Thompson Street in November 1939, so it wasn't surprising that children found the body of one of the building's more notorious residents. Joseph Piscitello had been shot three times with a large-caliber pistol and was dead in one of the hallways of the six-story tenement.[236]

Naturally, nobody in the crowded building, in which Rocco's restaurant occupied the ground floor, had anything to tell police about the incident. Still, detectives had a lot to work with to figure out who may have wanted Piscitello dead. First was the man's extensive arrest record, which included armed robbery, counterfeiting and assault. Clues on Piscitello's body could also prove useful in solving the crime. The man was well dressed, for one thing, raising the question of how he had earned (or perhaps printed) the money to pay for his expensive clothing. A diamond ring on one finger also indicated Piscitello had done well since serving a year and a day for the counterfeiting charge, but it was the gold watch on his wrist that detectives were most interested in. The watch bore the inscription "Margie to Joseph, November 25, 1939," the date just four days before Piscitello was shot and killed.[237]

The lady in question was one Margie Passantino, whom Piscitello had just become engaged to, the cops soon learned. Her address was unknown, but police were already tracking Passantino down. Their first question would be where she had gotten enough money to buy her fiancé such an expensive watch.[238]

3
THE 1940s

Visitors to the New York World's Fair of 1939 and 1940 had a foreboding sense that the world of tomorrow would involve Americans' entry into the war in Europe. The bombing of Pearl Harbor in December 1941 made that a reality, changing the lives of all Americans, especially Manhattanites. The island was a prime target for a possible attack by the Germans, and the U-boats in New York Harbor were cause for considerable concern. Soldiers and sailors, with money in their pockets, were everywhere, especially in the epicenters of Times Square, Broadway and Grand Central Terminal. New Yorkers were doing their patriotic part by enlisting and volunteering, whether that be by buying war bonds, donating blood, growing a victory garden, collecting scrap or serving as an air raid warden. The blackouts and rationing one had to endure were a small sacrifice compared to those serving and dying overseas. Even the mob was chipping in, ensuring that the docks it ran would not be sabotaged.

After the war, Manhattan emerged as a truly international city, with many of the best and brightest scientists, artists, journalists and playwrights now calling the place home. As symbolized by the new United Nations campus in east midtown, New York City was a world capital populated by leaders in business, art, fashion, finance, media and publishing. Heavily defined by ethnically distinct neighborhoods for the past century, Manhattan of the late forties was a more cosmopolitan place, the very essence of the American melting pot.

Lower Manhattan, 1941. *Rothstein, Arthur, photographer. Elevated structure and buildings. Lower Manhattan. New York United States, 1941. Dec. Photograph. https://www.loc.gov/item/2017774894/.*

Aerial view of Midtown Manhattan, 1945. *Aerial view of New York City / World Telegram & Sun photo by F. Palumbo. New York, 1945. [United States:] Photograph. https://www.loc.gov/item/2014648274/.*

There was a dark underbelly to this urban beast, however, both during and after the war. The world was in turmoil, after all, the cataclysmic event separating families and loved ones, sometimes permanently. Men and women in the armed forces away from their wives and husbands forged relationships, with some of those ending badly. The acute housing shortage added to the stress many felt, and racial tensions ran high despite our democratic ideals. And with lots of cash around, temptation proved to be too great for some not to take advantage of the situation, leading to one or more Manhattanites being pronounced dead on arrival.

FEELING FINE

Like her actor ex-husband, Burgess Meredith, Helen Derby Berrien Meredith's political ideology leaned decidedly left. As the daughter of the president of the American Cyanamid and Chemical Corporation, Meredith's liberal sentiments were off-putting to some in her social circle. The thirty-three-year-old woman also spent considerable time with friends who could be labeled "radical," a group not difficult to find near her five-room apartment on Washington Square.[239]

Oddly enough, it was these political beliefs that set in motion Meredith's suicide in April 1940. Meredith's current fiancé, a man named Kenneth Frank, whose occupation seemed unclear, disagreed strongly with her ideas and the like-minded people with whom she associated. Frank said as much in a letter he had recently sent her, citing this as the reason he would break off their engagement if she didn't change her views. Meredith chose a different course of action, turning on the jets of her gas stove in the kitchen of her spacious apartment. She left a note designating who should receive her money and furniture and had enough time to scribble one more line with a stubby pencil before expiring. "Feeling fine except for fumes," she hurriedly wrote on a kitchen calendar. Her body was found three hours later.[240]

FAT ELEVATOR

The Chip-Chip Boys were quite the sibling sextet. That was the nickname police used when referencing the six Reggione brothers, whose adult lives were committed to criminal activity of one kind or another. Given their destiny, the Chip-Chip Boys might have chosen other occupations. Mike Reggione was killed in 1933 for some offense, with James meeting a similar fate two years later. Patsy was in a Connecticut prison for burglary, and Tom was in Sing Sing for that same charge. John was apparently the golden child in the family, not wanted by the police for anything, which left Louis, who had served eight years in the pen for counterfeiting.[241]

In August 1940, Louis Reggione, who went by the fanciful sobriquet Fat Elevator for unknown reasons, was shot to death on Mulberry Street. Given the number of bullets fired at Fat Elevator (twelve), the forty-seven-year-old might have been considered lucky given that just five hit him. Still, that was enough to send Fat Elevator, who was wearing a light blue suit at the time, upstairs or, more likely, given his livelihood, downstairs. When the feds broke up his counterfeiting operation in 1932, they discovered that no less than $1 million in phony money had been printed and Fat Elevator was hiding from a party likely feeling that his piece of the pie was not quite large enough. Even though it was eight years later, certain types had excellent memories when big money (even if fake) was involved, making his previous business dealings the probable cause for his murder.[242]

THE SCIENTIST

At least he died doing what he loved, one might say, after learning of the strange death of Egbert Von Lepel. As usual, the sixty-year-old scientist was working in his private lab on West 60th Street on a Sunday in April 1941, experimenting with a high-frequency furnace being used by the U.S. Navy. Von Lepel was highly respected in the rather esoteric arena of electrical equipment, having invented something called the fixed quench high-frequency spark gap that was used almost universally until 1927, when it became obsolete.[243]

Even though it was Sunday, Von Lepel was busy in his lab, interested in how to possibly further speed up the modification of metals at high temperatures. While standing over a gas burner, however, the man suffered a seizure and, in falling, disconnected the tube. Fumes filled the room, making his death, unlike most involving gas, a regrettable accident.[244]

A KITCHEN POT

Coincidence or otherwise? Vesta Kelling, a feature writer for the Wide World News Service (part of the Associated Press), was dead in her apartment on East 52nd Street in December 1941 (just three days before the bombing of Pearl Harbor). The thirty-seven-year-old woman died in a gas explosion that blew out the windows of her apartment and woke up 150 other residents in the eighteen-story building. A flame under a kitchen pot had ignited two gas jets on the kitchen stove, Fire Marshal Thomas Brophy concluded after an investigation, raising the question of why two jets were open and why Kelling was using the stove when the blast occurred at 4:40 a.m.[245]

Also curious was the fact that Kelling had received a telegram the afternoon before the explosion informing her that her ex-husband had died suddenly in Lisbon. Newspaper reports did not specify how Lieutenant Colonel Charles M. Cummings, an Air Corps attaché at the U.S. Embassy in London, died, but it was certain that her former husband did not survive his trip back to this country. Was the explosion the result of a cooking accident or was Kellen too grief-stricken to go on?[246]

THE THIN MAN

The heavy-set rich lady suffocated, and her five-carat diamond ring and diamond pendant watch were missing. The plot of an Agatha Christie mystery? No, the real-life story of Marion Reich, or more accurately her real death story. In March 1942, the plump fifty-three-year-old wife of the head of a New Jersey manufacturing company was found bound and gagged in a suite at the Hotel Sutton on East 56th Street, the work of thieves who made off with her jewelry.[247]

Who done it? Police were after an individual they described as a "thin man" along with "a dark slender woman" who had registered at the hotel as Mr. and Mrs. Ted Leopold of Miami Beach (which turned out to be fictitious). The couple's only luggage was a paper box, this alone cause for some suspicion. It was their room in which the body of Mrs. Reich was found after she went to have lunch with Mrs. Leopold. No one, guest or staff, had seen Mrs. Reich at the hotel, however, something considered odd given that the woman was well over two hundred pounds and thus perhaps memorable. Nobody saw the registered couple leave the hotel, adding to the intrigue of the affair.[248]

Detectives looked for clues to try to solve the crime. They opened the door to the bedroom of the suite, only for it to be blocked by Mrs. Reich's body, which lay faced downward. A hard push of the door revealed that the woman's lips had been sealed with two-inch adhesive tape and, over that, a tightly wound paisley scarf. Her legs were bound with rubber-coated wire and her hands, lashed with the same wire, were behind her back. She was bruised in several places, suggesting that Mrs. Reich had not gone quietly into the night. A pair of pliers and an empty adhesive tape spool were found, but these were of no value in these pre–DNA analysis days.[249]

Still, there was a glimmer of hope of catching the elusive skinny couple. Hotel employees recognized a photo of a man pulled from the "rogues' gallery" at police headquarters, thinking it may be that of Ted Leopold. Duplicates of the photo were provided to one hundred detectives who were searching near and far for him and his equally lean partner.[250]

A MINOR COMPLICATION

In 1938, Mayor LaGuardia ordered that attendants replace medical interns on city ambulances, perhaps as a cost-saving measure or simply because there weren't enough interns to go around. (Interns completed medical school but had yet to receive their degree and license.) Whatever the reason, the mayor's decision created what a newspaper described as "a minor complication," specifically that the body of a dead person was not allowed to be removed for some time.[251]

One such complication involved Fred Seimers, the owner of a deli on 3rd Avenue near East 72nd Street, who attempted suicide in March 1942 by going to his basement and removing a plug from the gas pipe. A patrolman and another man smelled the fumes and entered the basement, only to be overcome themselves by the gas. A gas emergency crew along with Charles Carrithers, an ambulance attendant, arrived to try to save the fifty-six-year-old man through oxygen treatment. Carrithers and his ambulance soon left the scene, however, as he was convinced there was no hope for Seimers and he had no power to pronounce the man legally dead. It was only when a medical examiner was notified that the body of Seimers could be removed from the scene and taken to the morgue, an odd and disturbing situation. LaGuardia was a man of uncommon common sense, but his decision to take medical interns off of ambulances was not his best moment.[252]

A GREASE PIT

After getting married in a New London, Connecticut church in April 1942, Rocco Buscetto and Evelyn Christopher took the train to New York to spend their honeymoon. The couple spent a few days in the city, staying at the Hotel New Yorker, but it was time to get back to New London. The twenty-seven-year-old groom, a grocer, kissed his nineteen-year-old bride, telling her that he was going to Grand Central Terminal to get train tickets home. The man never came back.[253]

The following morning, the body of Buscetto was found in a grease pit at a gas station at West 57th Street and 11th Avenue. Police found no marks of violence on his body, but it did appear that the man's neck was broken. From the position of his body, it was clear that Buscetto had been murdered and then laid down carefully in the pit, rather than having been thrown or fallen in. The man had his hotel room key in his pocket, allowing police to locate his new wife and give her the news that her husband of a few days was dead. Although Buscetto's gold wedding band and gold watch remained on his body, robbery did appear to be the motive for the heinous crime. The man's wallet, which had contained sixty-two dollars, according to his wife, was gone, the likely reason he was killed.[254]

THE BARBERSHOP

If one didn't know better, it might have been a scene in an episode of *The Sopranos* or in a Martin Scorsese movie. But the story is entirely real, set in a SoHo barbershop in July 1942. Richard Percotti, a thirty-two-year-old unemployed truck driver, decided he needed a shave and headed to the Tunnel Barber Shop on 6th Avenue. Percotti, who had been arrested twice for stealing automobiles but was never convicted, sat in the first chair as the barber, Augustine Puluso, shaved the man. Suddenly, Puluso excused himself and went to the rear of the shop just as two men came through the front door. "Dick!" the men shouted to Percotti, who went by that name, and the man turned to see whom it was. One of the men fired a gun at Percotti, the bullet going into his head.[255]

Percotti was not dead, however, and he rose from the chair, left the shop and staggered outside. While the gunmen ran west across 6th Avenue to make their escape, Percotti reeled into a parked automobile and then fell dead on the sidewalk. Detectives had many questions for the barber and also interviewed Percotti's wife to see if she could shed any light on why her husband was murdered. Her husband had been "acting mysteriously" for the past year, she told the detectives, adding that despite being unemployed he had been buying and wearing new clothes.[256]

THE BRIDE-TO-BE

It was the plot of a Victorian melodrama or perhaps an operatic tragedy. A bride-to-be learns shortly before her marriage that her beloved fiancé is already married and, to really make readers or viewers teary-eyed, that he has had a child with said wife.[257]

A sad tale, certainly, especially since it's what really happened to Bernice Rose in September 1942. Rose, a twenty-seven-year-old widow, was deeply in love with "John" (no last name mentioned), and the couple had set an October wedding. But John was still married to another woman, he informed his betrothed a few days before their nuptials, and he had had a child with that woman. The fact that John was separated from his wife and that he had never even seen the child did not change things for Rose. The bride-to-be swallowed numerous sleeping tablets after checking into the Prince George Hotel on East 28th Street, where she was found dead in bed the following morning.[258]

Prince George Hotel (*left*), near Madison Square Park. *Irma and Paul Milstein Division of United States History, Local History and Genealogy, The New York Public Library. "Parks—Madison Square Park" New York Public Library Digital Collections. Accessed March 27, 2020. http://digitalcollections. nypl.org/items/510d47e2-c3a8-a3d9-e040-e00a18064a99.*

THE AIR RAID WARDEN

Since the bombing of Pearl Harbor and America's entry in World War II, George Wittkowsky had repeatedly tried to enlist. The army turned him down each time, however, as the forty-year-old man had some kind of "physical defect" that made him ineligible for military duty. To his credit, Wiitkowsky, who was a professor of business at City College, found a way to serve his country on the homefront. The man was an air raid warden, sometimes volunteering for all-night duty at the headquarters of Sector 3 on Washington Place.[259]

Wittkowsky's inability to serve overseas was apparently the reason why the man hanged himself in the middle of the night at the headquarters in October 1942. The following morning, Wittkowsky was found lying face-down on the floor; a broken rope was around his neck, its other end dangling from a pipe on the ceiling. A chair, which police believed he had stood on and then kicked away, was nearby. No notes were found, but the consensus was that it was the army's multiple rejections that led him to take his life.[260]

STRANGLED IN CENTRAL PARK

A woman was strangled in Central Park, making anyone who ventured into it, especially at night, more nervous than usual. Twenty-four-year-old Louise Almadovar was found dead in the northeast section of the park in November 1942, and police were already questioning five people at length in order to identify the murderer.[261]

The all-day interviews immediately revealed that this was likely no random killing. The dead woman's husband was the first to be brought in for questioning, and it was learned that the couple had recently separated. It was also gleaned that Mrs. Almadovar had not long ago beaten a woman with whom her husband had been friendly. Mr. Almadovar had danced with this other woman, something his wife was not too happy about since they were still married. The dead woman's father, who had threatened to beat his son-in-law for berating his daughter, was also being questioned. By the evening, the assistant district attorney booked Mr. Almadovar as a material witness, the initial step to perhaps charging the man with homicide.[262]

A POP

It was Christmas Eve 1942, and Louis Beyer, who ran a fish business, was in his office on South Street counting out $2,000 to be given as a bonus to his forty or so employees. Beyer heard "a pop" and ran down the wooden flight of stairs that led to the cashier's cage. There lay John Fannelli, a fish handler, with a single bullet between his eyes.[263]

Police were not sure why the twenty-eight-year-old man, who had worked for Beyer for seven years, was killed. Although dozens of workers were in and around the area of the shooting, none except Beyer himself had heard the gunshot, rather strangely, and nobody had seen the gunman. All of the employees made it clear to the police that no racketeering was taking place at the company, nor was there any labor dispute—despite each being common practices at the South Street Seaport at the time. With nothing else to go on, police were inclined to believe that the shooter was planning to rob Beyer for the Christmas bonus money and that Fannelli had attempted to stop him.[264]

South Street Seaport, 1933. *Historic American Buildings Survey, Creator. South Street Seaport Museum, New York County, NY. 1933. Documentation Compiled After. Photograph. https://www.loc. gov/item/ny0894/.*

A DUMBWAITER SHAFT

Who was the man who fell or perhaps was pushed down a dumbwaiter shaft on Hudson Street in January 1943? The man, who was estimated to be about thirty-five years old, carried various forms of identification, giving police his name and address. He was, according to a social security card and a selective service card, James Rogers Wills of Miami Beach and New York City.[265]

Upon reading a story about the incident, however, Wills made it quite clear that he had not fallen down a dumbwaiter shaft and was alive and well in Miami Beach working as a hotel chef. His wallet had been stolen a month earlier when in New York, he explained, making the thief most likely the dead person. Indeed, an examination of the dead man's fingerprints revealed him to be Francis McCarthy, alias Arthur McKinley, a petty thief wanted by the Boston police. It remained unclear how and why the thief had ended up at the bottom of a dumbwaiter shaft, but it likely had to do with the man's habit of taking things that did not belong to him.[266]

THE FIREMAN

John Sullivan was a fireman for twenty years, but he had been on sick leave for a month in September 1943. That's when his body, lying in a pool of blood, was found dead in the doorway of a plumbing store on 2nd Avenue at East 81st Street. Sullivan's head was bashed in, his right ear cut off and his face and body cut in a number of places.[267]

Who would want to murder a veteran fireman, and why? Police did not know, so they were tracing the man's movements on the last day of his life to find potential suspects. The forty-nine-year-old had quite a busy day, as it turned out. The man left his apartment at 11:00 a.m., telling his wife that he'd be back in about an hour. Instead, Sullivan visited a number of bars in the neighborhood over the course of the afternoon, ending up at the 84th Street station of the 3rd Avenue El. It was there that the man decided to throw bottles down to the street, raising the possibility that the killer was someone who had been on the receiving end of Sullivan's projectile flinging. Twenty-five detectives assigned to the case questioned thirty persons to determine if it was that or if something deeper was behind the odd episode.[268]

THE PICKPOCKET

While waiting for a train at the 103rd Street station of the IRT subway in January 1944, Joseph Bruno felt himself get jostled by two men. Bruno realized the men were trying to take his wallet, and a scuffle broke out. A fourth man, trying to help out Bruno, who was now shouting, got into the action, and the station agent saw and heard the kerfuffle and called the subway police.[269]

Upon seeing the police arrive, the pair of pickpockets fled in separate directions, one north and one south. The one who headed south chose to run on the tracks, which turned out to be an unwise decision. He got as far as 100th Street, when an oncoming train struck and killed him. The conductor had not seen the man but did stop the train when he felt a "bump" in the back. The pickpocket was identified as William Maher, who had been arrested just ten days earlier for "jostling" a passenger on a subway train. Bruno's wallet, which contained $100, had been dropped at some point by one of the two men and was recovered.[270]

GOD FORGIVE ME

Committing suicide by suffocation is difficult and rare, but police had no other explanation for how Helen Oetjen died. In February 1944, the thirty-nine-year-old ex-vaudeville dancer was found dead in her apartment on East End Avenue near 83rd Street, her mouth sealed with six wide strips of adhesive tape and her nostrils stuffed with cotton.[271]

Coming upon such a scene would almost always lead detectives to believe a murder had taken place. But in this case, a note had been left, with all indications that it was suicide. The note, which read, "God Forgive Me," was signed "Helen" and, more important, was in Oetjen's handwriting. The woman held a rosary in her hands, another sign that she had taken her own life, and it was learned that she was being treated for heart disease. Still, an autopsy was planned to determine the precise cause of death and, with that information, solve the mystery.[272]

7-F

It was a particularly ugly scene at one of the city's most frequented spots. In August 1944, a young woman lay dead in a clump of bushes right near the main door of the Hayden Planetarium at West 81st Street and Central Park West. Detectives could tell right away that she had been strangled. The body had been found by a couple of Park Department workmen, who initially believed that what they came upon in the rhododendrons and other ornamental shrubs was a heap of newspapers. Hundreds of people had no doubt passed by her body without realizing it was a human being. Although the woman was taken to the morgue around noon, her identification remained unknown at midnight. An apartment key labeled "7-F" was discovered in the woman's clothes, not much to go on. Based on the condition of her face and her clothing, it was clear that the woman had been beaten up before she was killed, adding to the lurid nature of the case.[273]

More facts released about the mystery woman fueled the public's interest. She was blond and in her late twenties, likely attractive before being pummeled and choked to death. Her hair and nails were well kept, police informed reporters, and her clothing was of high quality. An undergarment was found in her handbag, infusing a dose of sexuality to the crime. That the very spot where the woman was discovered was known as a rendezvous for amorous couples further made it appear that the murder was a result of a romantic entanglement gone horribly wrong.[274]

The plot thickened a few days later when the victim was positively identified. She was Phyllis Newmark, who lived with her husband on West 79th Street, just a couple of blocks where she was almost certainly killed.

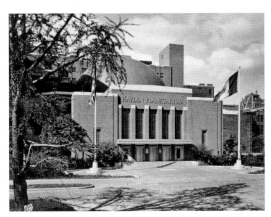

Hayden Planetarium. *Irma and Paul Milstein Division of United States History, Local History and Genealogy, The New York Public Library. "West 81st Street–Central Park West" New York Public Library Digital Collections. Accessed March 27, 2020. http://digitalcollections.nypl.org/items/510d47e2-cfbe-a3d9-e040-e00a18064a99.*

A major windfall for detectives was a little address book found in her apartment. Dozens of people listed in the book were being questioned to determine if they had anything to do with her death. After he admitted to having enjoyed Newmark's company a couple of years earlier, one man, an ex-sailor who had been dishonorably discharged from the navy, was being held as a material witness. This wasn't nearly enough to convict or even formally charge the man, however, and detectives confessed they were hoping for a "lucky break" to learn who had murdered Newmark.[275]

MY HUSBAND HAS BEEN KILLED!

A wealthy man was dead in a penthouse apartment that had been ransacked. A jewel case had been forced open, and several pieces were missing. The man's wife was screaming, "My husband has been killed!" Could one ask for a more sensational story?[276]

It was Ben Lewis, brother of Nat Lewis, the notable Broadway clothier, who was dead in his apartment on East 53rd Street in November 1944. The man's wife found the body of her fifty-one-year-old husband on the bed, her pilfered jewel case next to him. Desk drawers had been pulled out, their contents scattered about, and the liquor cabinet had been opened and raided. Chairs on the terrace were overturned, adding to the general mayhem.[277]

Detectives put the pieces of the puzzle together. Lewis, who worked at his brother's company, closed the store at 10:00 p.m. and arrived home half an hour later. An examination of his body showed no signs of violence, suggesting that Lewis had entered the apartment as the burglary was taking place. Surprised, to say the least, Lewis had a heart attack, they believed, making this a case of being literally frightened to death, and thus, in a sense, manslaughter. An autopsy was planned to definitively determine the cause of death.[278]

THE STEVEDORE

For whatever reason, Thomas Gleason liked to spend time in the reception room of a Hell's Kitchen funeral home. One day in December 1944, the forty-five-year-old stevedore (a dockworker who loads and unloads cargo from ships) was seated in his usual chair at the Thomas P. Madine Funeral Parlor on 10th Avenue near West 46th Street. Gleason was talking with the parlor's caretaker when the latter left the room and another man holding a gun entered. The man shot Gleason once through the forehead, once in the left side of his head and once in the chest, just above the heart. Powder burns remained on Gleason's body, meaning the rounds were fired at close range.[279]

Why would someone want to assassinate someone else in a funeral parlor? History was, in a sense, repeating itself. About five years earlier, Gleason's business partner, a Mr. Beadle, was killed in a similar fashion just a few yards away. Gleason, Beadle and a third partner had worked the Hudson River piers, leading police to believe that each murder was connected to a cargo-related dispute going years back.[280]

THE BLIND STUDENT

Louis Henderson was a remarkable person by any measure. The twenty-two-year-old from Minneapolis was working toward his doctorate at Columbia University, having already earned a master's degree at the University of Chicago. Henderson had also taught Far Eastern foreign affairs at the Army Civil Affairs Training School in Chicago, quite a thing given that most people his age had not yet earned a college degree, if they went to college at all.[281]

Henderson's achievements were all the more impressive given that the young man was blind. That condition may have made others socially withdrawn, but Henderson was among the most popular graduate students at the university. Classmates often typed up Henderson's papers, and the university provided him with a private room in the Warren Hall Residence Club on West 115th Street to study without the usual collegiate merriment.[282]

All of this was made all the more tragic by Henderson's suicide in January 1945. When a friend who came to Henderson's room could not rouse him, the manager of the club used his passkey and found him dead. Henderson had inhaled ether from a one-pound can, leaving two notes written in braille.[283]

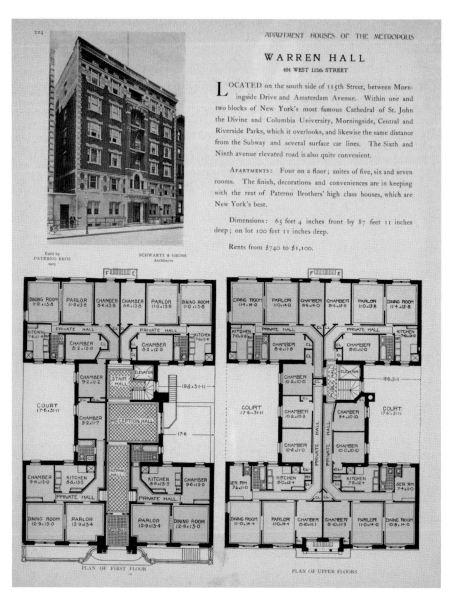

Plan for Warren Hall Residence at Columbia University. *Irma and Paul Milstein Division of United States History, Local History and Genealogy, The New York Public Library. "Warren Hall, 404 West 115th Street; Plan of first floor; Plan of upper floors." New York Public Library Digital Collections. Accessed March 27, 2020. http://digitalcollections.nypl.org/items/510d47db-9f6d-a3d9-e040-e00a18064a99.*

THE ELEVATOR MURDER

Newspapers were calling it "the elevator murder." In March 1945, Salvatore Bianco was entering an automatic lift in an apartment building on East 16th Street near Avenue A when a series of shots rang out. The forty-four-year-old man fell, seven bullets in his head and chest fired from at least two revolvers (a .32 and a .38). For some reason, one of the killers then pressed a button of the elevator, taking the already dead man to the second floor. There the door opened and Bianco's body spilled out. Police were on the lookout for three gunmen who escaped in an automobile, in which they sped west on East 15th Street and then north on 1st Avenue.[284]

While the hit men were on the loose, detectives' first order of business was figuring out their motive. Robbery was ruled out, as Bianco, a woman's coat manufacturer and part-time undertaker, had $1,160.84 in his pockets. The man had no police record and was not involved in any rackets, although no one could explain what Bianco was doing in that part of town since he neither worked nor lived there. The man was married, but his wife and two children were in Sicily, where they had traveled five years earlier and could not leave because of the war.[285]

Detectives realized they were onto something when they learned that Bianco was an acquaintance of Philippo Rappa, also a coat manufacturer, who was found dead in Queens four months earlier. Bianco lived just two miles from where Rappa's body was discovered, more reason to believe there was a connection between the two dead men and their deaths. Police were still working on the Rappa case, as it was not clear how he died. An autopsy revealed that the actual cause of death was drowning, but the man also had a two-inch gash on the back of his head, suggesting foul play may have been involved.[286]

SOMEONE IN HERE

Sergeant Malick Vessaf survived World War II only to be killed in a YMCA hotel a couple of months after V-J Day. Vessaf, a career soldier based at Fort Dix, was found dead at Sloane House, the YMCA hotel at West 34th Street, in October 1945. Repeated blows of a twelve-pound water hose nozzle had crushed his head.[287]

When the fifty-year-old man checked into the hotel, he left a large envelope containing certain valuables at the front desk. Vessaf checked out of his single room after a couple days but returned the next day, only to learn that only double rooms were available. Vessaf went in search of someone to share the room, which proved to be a fatal decision. He returned with a man who registered as "Sgt. James Post, Waterford, N.Y.," who police believed to be Vessaf's killer.[288]

Suspicion began to be raised when maids intending to clean the room were repeatedly barred entry and told, "Someone in here." Finally, a maid further up the chain of command entered the room and saw the dead Sergeant Vessaf. The man's shoes, army jacket and identification tags were missing from his body and the room, leading police to a theory of what had taken place. "Sgt. James Post" murdered Vessaf for the valuables and, bloodied from the act, swapped his clothes for his own. The ID tags could help the killer pass off as Vessaf, a key asset if the latter's valuables included negotiable paper. No "Sgt. James Post" had yet to be located in Waterford, military or civilian, not surprisingly, and Vessaf had no next of kin to notify of his unfortunate death.[289]

GET OVER HERE RIGHT AWAY

"Get over here right away," Lieutenant (jg) Pauline Rupp of the U.S. Marine Corps told her friend, a physician at Bellevue Hospital, on the phone in October 1945. Rupp was calling about the condition of the man in her room at the Governor Clinton Hotel at West 31st Street and 7th Avenue, which was not good. The physician called police, and by the time they arrived, Lieutenant John Mooney was dead. A medical examiner could not determine the exact cause of death of the navy man, but several bottles of a medicine were found in the room, suggesting poisoning.[290]

Adding to the puzzle was that Lieutenant Rupp, who herself was either a doctor or a nurse, was unconscious and in critical condition. Detectives theorized that the two had taken the drugs as part of a suicide pact, but only an autopsy of Mooney and examination of Rupp would provide more clues about what had happened.[291]

LOCAL TRADE ROW

Irving Weiss died where he had spent much of the past six years, his liquor store on Christopher Street. Found in a sitting position behind his swivel chair, surrounded by cartons of liquor, Weiss had two bullets in the left side of his head and two in the left forearm. Whoever had shot and killed the forty-year-old man in January 1946, he had to be virtually touching Weiss when he fired his gun. Powder burns were on the deceased's arm, an indication he had tried to stop the bullets from hitting him.[292]

Liquor store holdups were common in Manhattan, and Weiss had in fact been robbed twice in such a manner since 1940. But this is not how he died, police concluded after finding eighty-five dollars in cash on his desk and another thirty or so in the register. Rather, it was a competitor who shot and killed the man, detectives believed, having some knowledge there was a "local trade row" going on among liquor store owners in the area. As usual, no one heard or saw anything.[293]

THE SWITCHBLADE

Sidney McHeath was a bad guy. The twenty-eight-year-old man assaulted his live-in girlfriend on a number of occasions, and one day in January 1946 he attacked a tenant in his building on Bradhurst Avenue in Harlem with a switchblade knife. It was time to bring McHeath in, and two detectives accompanied by three cops in uniform went to his apartment to do just that.[294]

McHeath made a run for it when the police arrived, but the man was soon found in a closet in another tenant's apartment. Even though he was outnumbered, McHeath did not go easily; it took twenty minutes for the five officers to subdue him and get him into the police car and then to the West 135th Street Station. McHeath was placed in a holding room with a glass panel door. Suddenly, the man burst through the door, the switchblade in his hand. McHeath charged directly at one of the arresting officers, Detective Franz, while the other cops and the suspect's girlfriend, who was there pressing charges, watched in horror. Cool as a cucumber, Franz drew his service revolver and, just as McHeath was about to stab the detective, shot the man. An ambulance was called, but McHeath was already dead.[295]

A FAMILIAR FIGURE

Central Park was proving its reputation as a dangerous place to be after dark, even for war veterans. (There was an after-midnight curfew, but it was widely violated.) A twenty-year-old female former member of the Army Air Forces was killed in June 1946, and a month later an ex-soldier was found dead just inside the park entrance at West 61st Street and Central Park West. The latter case was a mysterious one. Twenty-nine-year-old Francis Hedges, considered a "familiar figure" in that part of the park, was dead from a bullet wound in his right temple, a classic sign of suicide.[296]

Detectives weren't so sure, however. First of all, where was the gun? Police searched nearby shrubs and paths but found nothing, a curious thing. Second, while there were a few powder marks on the man's head, the bullet entry point was not what was called a "contact" wound. This meant that the gun was not touching or very close to his head when it went off, further discounting the suicide theory.[297]

One of two very different things happened, detectives were thinking. The first possibility was that Hedges held the gun quite a distance from his head when it fired, and then somebody took the .32, explaining why it could not be found. The other possibility was that somebody else shot the man from a distance, and the killer took the gun with him. While detectives pondered the two scenarios, extra policemen were assigned to the park to more diligently enforce the after midnight curfew.[298]

A PARTLY FILLED BATHTUB

The circumstances attached to the death of a woman who lived on the fifteenth floor of Prospect Tower in Tudor City were not clear. In March 1947, sixty-seven-year-old Florence Denton was found slashed to death in a partly filled bathtub in her apartment, with the scene a particularly grisly one. On her body underneath her negligee and bathrobe were a number of bruises and razorblade cuts, although it was difficult to tell whether these were self-inflicted. A bruise and deep cut over one eye seemed odd for a suicide victim to have, and a knocked over lamp and other disturbances in the apartment suggested that a struggle had recently taken place. As well, razor blades were scattered throughout the apartment, and there were bloodstained towels and clothing in the bathroom.[299]

As typical in such cases, police looked first to the victim's husband for answers. Mr. Denton found his wife's body and called the police, but the doctor examining the body could not determine the exact cause of her death until an autopsy was performed. That doctor happened to be the family physician, who reported having treated Mrs. Denton just two weeks earlier for a wound on her forehead.[300]

AN ORANGE BATH TOWEL

It was classic film noir, which was all the rage at the time, except it was real. A former motion picture actress was dead, having been strangled with a bedsheet. The killer was someone who Sheila Mannering knew, police were certain, although that left open dozens of possibilities.[301]

The scene in Mannering's apartment on West 57th Street in July 1947 was indeed a disturbing one. Mannering, who had starred in a handful of silent movies in the 1920s (as Bessie True) and had also done some radio work, was found nude and lying diagonally on the floor of her bedroom. The sheet was knotted around the forty-nine-year-old woman's neck, and an orange bath towel was stuffed into her mouth. A lamp had been overturned, and a two-inch butt of a freshly smoked cigar remained in an ashtray. Two slight contusions were visible on Mannering's chin, made by someone wearing a ring, detectives believed. The woman had been dead twelve to twenty-four hours, according to Medical Examiner Henry Siegel, the cause of death asphyxiation from strangulation.[302]

The Police Department was not treating this as an ordinary murder, although of course there was no such thing. An intensive investigation was underway, led by none other than Police Commissioner Arthur Wallander, Chief Inspector Martin Brown and Deputy Chief Inspector Edward Mullins. Mannering had been throttled in the morning, but by midnight these three had personally questioned more than 25 people, all but one of them men. Sixty detectives were on the case and interrogated an additional 150 persons, but no suspects had yet been produced. Mannering had not worked in years, making detectives wonder how she could her afford her $87.50 a month apartment ($1,000.00 today) and a part-time maid, who had discovered her body. The woman also owned a Tiffany's wristwatch, a number of rings, and had $52.00 in cash in her apartment, not to mention a receipt for two mink coats that were in storage. Robbery was definitely not the motive, police had already concluded, convinced that her brutal slaying was of a much more personal nature.[303]

THE PIANIST

Who'd want to kill a Greenwich Village piano teacher? Or had Victor Trerice killed himself? Police didn't know, as there were signs of both murder and suicide. The body of the forty-year man was found on a rumpled bed amid overturned furniture in his basement apartment on Grove Street in March 1948, and there was more evidence there had been a fight. Both of Trerice's eyes were blackened, and there was a gash over the right one.[304]

But Trerice had not died from those injuries. Rather, it was that five gas jets were open in the kitchen, with all indications that is how the man had perished. Trerice's wife lived somewhere upstate, making her the next of kin, who police had to notify and, because of the mysterious circumstances, question.[305]

THOSE WHO ARE ENAMORED BY DEATH

Jack De Moreland, a poet, was a "failure," he told a friend early one morning in September 1948, leaving his friend's apartment on Bank Street in a depressed state. Moments later, his friend heard a crash and looked out a window. It was De Moreland, who had jumped off the roof of the five-story building. Fittingly, perhaps, De Moreland's suicide attempt was a complete failure. The thirty-year-old man hit the canopy of the building's entrance on the way down and then fell softly onto the roof of a car parked a few feet away. De Moreland's friend frantically called police, but when he returned to the window, De Moreland was gone, completely unscathed.[306]

De Moreland then went uptown to another friend's apartment on East 107th Street, where he was staying. He tied a piece a rope to an overhead pipe and successfully hanged himself. Police found about fifteen poems in the apartment, one of them reading:

> *The drawing together of Jupiter and the moon and harvest equals God reaping the dead of the moon—those who are enamored by death.*[307]

THE VIOLINIST

On summer evenings, Ignatz Diaczuk, a tailor, often entertained neighborhood children by playing the violin on the doorstep of his shop on East 10th Street. The sixty-seven-year-old man who immigrated to the United States from the Ukraine in 1903 also played his violin at the nearby Russo-Carpathian Orthodox Church, and he also happened to have an artificial right leg.[308]

Not exactly whom one would consider a prime target for homicide, Diaczuk was strangled in the back of his shop on East 10th Street in September 1948. Robbery was not the motive, as the man's watch and chain were found on him, and he had money in his pocket. Detectives went to Diaczuk's apartment at the back of the shop, and there they found a possible clue to his murder. Hanging on nails in the bedroom was a violin bearing the label "Stradivarius 1730" and another violin that was a German copy of an Amati. The violins were highly valuable, raising the possibility that the murderer had not had the chance to find the instruments and thus killed Diaczuk for literally nothing.[309]

4
THE 1950s

Mid-twentieth-century Manhattan was a wonderland—anyone who was there at the time will tell you. With New York City emerging as the undisputed capital of the world after the war, the island became a mecca in the 1950s for Americans and foreigners alike. While folkies, the Beats and beboppers did their respective thing, men in gray flannel suits ran America and much else of the world. Midtown was an especially exciting part of town. "Mad men" worked and played hard on Madison Avenue, swingers swung on Swing (52nd) Street and it was the Golden Age of Broadway.

Manhattan in the fifties was a buzzing beehive of both intellectualism and aestheticism. In a single day, one could listen to Thelonious Monk at the Five Spot, groove with Jack Kerouac at a café on Bleecker Street, muse over the new abstract expressionism paintings at the Museum of Modern Art and then take in a foreign film at an artsy cinematique. Times Square had yet to be Disneyfied, of course, so the area was filled with hedonistic delights for the more adventurous, including naughty movies, strip clubs and dive bars. New York was an even later night town these days; it was not unusual for middle-aged folks to stay out until 2:00 or 3:00 a.m.

Alongside this celebration of life was the disturbing feeling that it could end at any moment. Anxieties ran high during the heyday of the Cold War, and anti-communism fever only added to the sense that Big Brother was watching whatever one did. The abundant society of the postwar years was dangled as a refuge from such worries, the dominant narrative being to keep up with the Joneses and grab one's piece of the American pie. Still, many could not escape

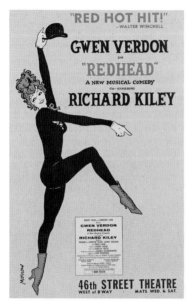 

Left: Poster for the 1959 Broadway show *Redhead*, which won a number of Tony Awards. *Billy Rose Theatre Division, The New York Public Library. "Poster for the Broadway stage production Redhead." New York Public Library Digital Collections. Accessed March 27, 2020. http:// digitalcollections.nypl.org/items/6ac6c280-74c8-0131-f1d6-58d385a7bbd0.*

Right: Poster for the 1956 Broadway show *Pipe Dream*, a musical by Richard Rodgers and Oscar Hammerstein II. *Billy Rose Theatre Division, The New York Public Library. "Rodgers & Hammerstein present Helen Traubel William Johnson in a new musical Pipe Dream co-starring Judy Tyler..." New York Public Library Digital Collections. Accessed March 27, 2020. http://digitalcollections. nypl.org/items/7c959756-46a0-7938-e040-e00a18066450.*

the existential angst that defined these years and the significant pressure to conform to social norms. Was it any wonder that such bottled-up emotions occasionally exploded, leaving a Manhattanite dead on arrival?

A HAMMER AND A BRICK

Her skull had been crushed, and a hammer and a brick lay near her body. Rosa Blancke was dead in her apartment in the brownstone she owned on West 120th Street in January 1951. As she was found in a dirty housedress and an old brown sweater, one might believe that it would not be worth robbing the sixty-five-year-old woman. But Blancke had a good income from renting out rooms in her building, and she was involved in a variety of other businesses that made her a relatively wealthy woman. The new television set and electric refrigerator in her cluttered apartment were signs that Blancke was rolling in dough.[310]

At least one scoundrel could tell that when it came to the old lady in the old clothes, appearances were deceiving. He or they entered her apartment around 2:30 a.m. and delivered heavy blows to her head with the hammer and brick. The killer(s) were twenty-four hours too late, however, taking maybe $70 she had in the apartment. The day before, Blancke had deposited $3,250 in cash at the Manufacturers Trust Company bank, a figure worth ten times that amount today.[311]

THE HAIRDRESSER

Until a few months prior, John Bevilacqua had been a hairdresser at Wanamaker's department store. Nice work if you can get it, but the thirty-nine-year-old man had decided to pursue another, more lucrative venture. Bevilacqua, who lived with his parents in Brooklyn, was part of a stolen automobile ring and, judging by appearances, was doing quite well in it. He wore jewelry, drove a Cadillac and carried large sums of cash around, some of it spent at the nightclubs on Broadway he liked to frequent.[312]

Bevilacqua's good run came to a sudden end in November 1951, however, when he was shot dead in the hallway of a tenement on West 25th Street. Bevilacqua registered at the Hotel New Yorker at 3:30 a.m. as "Frank Bello" and got a phone call an hour later, presumably to arrange a meeting. He proceeded to the building on West 25th Street, where four bullets were promptly put into his head. Somebody crossed somebody in the buying and selling of stolen automobiles, it can be assumed, suggesting that Bevilacqua should have kept his cushy if not great paying job cutting and styling hair for rich old ladies.[313]

THE DRESS MAN

One day in February 1952, Nathan Nelson was late for an appointment with his brother and another man with whom Nelson worked at the Advance Junior Dress Company. The two repeatedly called Nelson at his home on

West 55th Street, but there was no answer, reason for concern. The men made their way to the apartment but, even with a key, could not open the door. Nelson's brother climbed a fire escape to the fourth-floor apartment and entered through a bathroom window.[314]

Nelson was dead on the living room floor of his "bachelor" apartment, having been shot at close range in the stomach and mouth. A struggle had definitely taken place, police determined. Furniture was upset, and Nelson's clothes were disheveled and torn. There was no sign of the thirty-seven-year-old man's wallet or his .38-caliber revolver, for which he had a permit. Detectives considered possible reasons why Nelson had been killed and robbed. Besides being in the schmatta business, the man was a partner in a dress trucking concern, making this a line of inquiry alongside his personal life.[315]

A DANGEROUS LUNATIC

News of a murder was always alarming, but this was truly shocking. In July 1952, twenty-year-old Eileen Fahey was shot dead by an unidentified man in a room on the ninth floor of the Pupin Building of Columbia University at Broadway and 120th Street. For two years, Fahey had worked as a secretary and bookkeeper for the American Physical Society. The killer strolled away from the scene, a crime so upsetting that it made the front page of the *New York Times*.[316]

Soon, however, the perpetrator was arrested. He was Bayard Peakes, a twenty-nine-year-old "pseudo-physicist" and Air Force veteran who had authored an electronic theory that nobody had taken seriously. Peakes confessed to the crime after being picked up in Boston by New York detectives who had been on his trail since the shooting.[317] After Peakes was charged with murder in the first degree, the court committed him to Bellevue Hospital for observation. Meanwhile, the parents of the young woman were filing a lawsuit against the Army and Veteran's Administration for allowing Peakes to be there in the first place. Employees there knew he was a "dangerous lunatic," the petition stated, and were thus at fault for allowing the man to remain at large among "an unsuspecting public."[318]

A BOX OF PAJAMAS

It's not clear what Ernest Cade thought was in the box that he decided to take from a truck at 10th Avenue and West 37th Street in May 1953, but had he lived, he'd most likely have been disappointed. The nineteen-year-old man climbed to the cab roof of a truck parked there, untied the corner of a tarpaulin covering the load and grabbed a package and threw it to the ground. He then walked north along 10th Avenue with the package on his shoulder.[319]

Regrettably for Cade, three detectives had observed the whole thing and began to follow him. Cade turned a corner and began walking east on West 38th Street, which is when one of the detectives flashed his badge and ordered him to stop. Cade spun around and started running, passing the other two detectives on the way. They too shouted at him to halt. Instead, Cade dropped the package and dashed through traffic on 10th Avenue. Each of those two detectives fired a shot, with one of them striking Cade in the neck. He was pronounced dead at the scene. The truck driver went to the West 30th Street police station to retrieve the package, which turned out to be a box of nylon pajamas.[320]

THE CHINESE IMPORTER

Stephen Wang was dead, and he likely knew his assailant, as there were no signs of a struggle. The fifty-one-year-old Chinese importer and proprietor of an Oriental goods store on Second Avenue was shot five times in the rear of his shop in September 1953.[321]

Police already had a prime suspect in mind: an unnamed seaman who had wanted to marry Wang's daughter Jo Ann. As in a Shakespearean tragedy, perhaps, Wang objected, and forbid his daughter to see the sailor. The rejected suitor had been seen near Wang's store shortly before his body was discovered, however, leading police to believe he was the likely gunman.[322]

I COULDN'T DO IT ALONE

It was as disturbing a suicide as they come. Two nineteen-year-old women had tried to kill themselves in New Jersey one afternoon in July 1954 and, when that attempt failed, partly succeeded that evening in Manhattan. One woman, Madeline Sommer, was found dead from gas poisoning at an art gallery/apartment on East 65th Street, while the other, Helene Jacobs, was found unconscious and in critical condition. Earlier in the day, the women turned on the gas at Sommer's New Jersey home, but all it did was set fire to the house. The blaze was extinguished and had done little damage, but the women's plans remained the same. They took a cab to a friend's gallery/apartment, drank a bottle and a half of wine and turned on the gas. The building's superintendent and a repairman entered the place and found the pair, rescuing the moaning Jacobs just in time.[323]

The two women, juniors at Syracuse University, were excellent students and appeared to be happy. Sommer had been planning to enter Yale University after graduating, and Jacobs was enrolled at Barnard College for graduate work. Their suicide notes painted a different picture, however. Sommer's note explained that she was dissatisfied with life, while Jacobs wrote that she hadn't "enough life to nourish myself through long, long years." Sommer seemed to be the protagonist in the sad story. "I couldn't do it alone, so I am taking Helene with me," her note said.[324]

A CREAM-COLORED CAR

The killers were either thoughtful or had a sense of humor. The gangsters had taken Salvatore La Scala for the "last ride" their type was famous for but parked the automobile that contained his body right in front of an undertaking establishment on Sullivan Street.[325]

La Scala was free on bail in January 1955 on the charge of receiving stolen goods, specifically furs, but in retrospect the thirty-year-old man should have stayed in jail. He had two bullets in his head, another sign that it was the work of mobsters who felt they had been wronged in some way. La Scala had in fact been arrested with six other persons, raising the possibility that the man had or had plans to squeal on his thieving colleagues. Certainly upset about the situation was one Vincent Mulo of Brooklyn, who had lent his new cream-colored car to La Scala; he could not return it.[326]

THE ARMS OF HIS WIFE

Sergeant First Class Enrique Garcia was a student at the Army Language School in Monterey, California, in January 1956. His wife had recently left him, taking their two-year-old daughter with her back to relatives at the East River Houses development at East 105th Street. The twenty-eight-year-old, who had been in the U.S. Army for eight years, left the school without clearance and then sold his television set and some furniture. He used the money to buy an airplane ticket to New York and a .32-caliber pistol.[327]

Garcia made his way to the housing complex and hid in a downstairs hallway. After grocery shopping, Carmen, the man's wife, returned to the building and entered the elevator, their daughter in her arms. Garcia grabbed the child from the arms of his wife and fired six shots at her. She fell dead, and the girl was unharmed. Garcia then took the child to the fifth-floor apartment of his wife's cousin and handed the girl to her. The sergeant ran two blocks from the scene when police in a squad car stopped him. Garcia told police of the shooting and handed them his pistol. He was held on a charge of homicide.[328]

THE LIBRARIAN

Alfred Kilbourne Hammer Jr., a theological seminary librarian, was fascinated by the art and practice of hanging. He even owned a book on the subject, Charles Duff's *A New Handbook of Hanging* (whose catchy subtitle is "Being a short introduction to the fine art of execution, containing much useful information on neck-breaking, throttling, strangling, asphyxiation, decapitation and electrocution for hangmen, and many other items of interest.") The book was inscribed, having been gifted to him.[329]

So perhaps it wasn't surprising that the red-haired, stocky twenty-seven-year-old was found hanging by a rope from the top hinge of a closet door in his apartment on Columbus Avenue between West 106th and West 107th Streets in September 1956. There was just one catch: a pillowcase was around Hammer's neck, a rope bound his hands behind his back and his mouth had been sealed with tape.[330]

Given that, Deputy Chief Inspector Edward Byrnes was starting his investigation with the theory that Hammer, who worked at the General Theological Seminary, was murdered. Byrnes gathered some background material on Hammer to help solve the crime, assuming there was one. The man was brilliant and hardworking, his colleagues reported, and he had never missed a day of work. Hammer also served as an acolyte at the Protestant Episcopal Church of St. Mary the Virgin on West 46th Street. Interestingly, until just a week or two earlier, Hammer had shared his apartment with another man. Byrnes was also following up on a report that, according to one person, Hammer "was supposed to have tried something along these lines to see what it would feel like."[331]

THE DIVORCEE

Vera King had met a violent end, but that's about all police could say when her body was found in her apartment on West End Avenue near West 87th Street in December 1956. One side of her face was bruised, enough evidence to list the fifty-two-year-old woman's death as suspicious.[332]

King, a former showgirl, was described in newspaper reports as a "divorcee," much in part due to the position of her ex-husband, Milton Kramer. Milton Kramer was the son of Max Kramer, who had built numerous hotels, theaters and apartment houses and had died a decade earlier. She and Milton Kramer had divorced just six months earlier in Paris, adding to the intrigue around her death. Ironically, a former city detective had been in King's apartment the day she was likely murdered. He had spent the night there and left in the morning, reporting that she was very much alive at that point. When he returned that afternoon, however, she was dead, suspicious indeed.[333]

A LOT OF DRUGS

Two men were found dead in a hotel room in strange circumstances one afternoon in August 1957. It was not an ordinary hotel room, and they were not ordinary men. The pair was staying in a five-room suite in the Sulgrave Hotel on Park Avenue at East 67th Street, quite the fancy digs in the fanciest part of town. One of the men was Orville Harden, a sixty-three-year-old retired vice president–director of the Standard Oil Company, and the other man was thirty-one-year-old David Lyon, the son of a New Jersey physician.[334]

The police and a medical examiner could not determine how the men had died. There were no visible wounds on their bodies or signs of violence. There were, however, "a lot of drugs," according to detectives after searching the room, notably a half-empty bottle of paraldehyde, which was commonly used in the treatment of alcoholism, as well as an assortment of tranquilizers and sedatives. There were also numerous hypodermic needles, more evidence that at least one of the men was using drugs.[335]

As the medical examiner performed autopsies to determine the causes of death, police tried to make sense of the peculiar scene. Lyon had known Harden for seven years, they learned, and he often stayed with the older man. Harden was using the hotel room as his permanent address, although he had a winter home in Miami as well. He and Lyon had stayed at that home until June, in fact, when they, along with a third man, came to New York. The third man was Robert Allman, a thirty-three-year-old unemployed artist who had been discharged from the Navy. (Allman and Lyon had been classmates at an arts school in New York.) Why was Harden—one of the world's foremost authorities on the oil business, recipient of the Order of Commander in the French Legion of Honor, and a member of the Knickerbocker and Links Clubs—spending much of his time with these two men?[336]

The autopsy results provided some answers but not nearly enough to answer that question. The two men died of "general visceral congestion," according to the medical examiner, medicalese for a failure of one of more internal organs. Next step was a chemical analysis of the vital organs, especially the heart, liver and intestines, by Dr. Alexander Gettler, the city toxicologist, to try to establish exact cause of death. While that avenue was explored, detectives located and grilled Allman for ten hours. Lyon had gone to his parents' home in New Jersey when they arrived in New York from Miami, Allman explained, but he stayed with Harden in the hotel. Harden, who had heart trouble, paid Allman $70 a week to take care of him, but he had left about a week earlier because, in his words, he "couldn't stand Mr. Harden's drinking." (This despite the fact that Allman was found at 4:00 a.m. in a West Side bar.) Allman had observed the two taking the paraldehyde, and he was aware that Lyon came to the hotel after he left. That was all the information he provided to police despite the lengthy questioning, however, leaving things in considerable confusion.[337]

THE BROTHER

His brother had fallen or jumped from their hotel window, Charles Glinton told police in September 1957 after a man's body was found on the ground. Indeed, it appeared that Howard Glinton had either accidently tumbled out a fifth-floor window of the Hotel Marie Antoinette on Broadway at West 66th Street or had committed suicide, leading police to close the case.[338]

A couple of months later, however, it was learned that the dead man was not Charles Glinton's brother, and the man had been pushed out the window. Charles Glinton, a thirty-three-year-old short-order cook, was charged with the murder of Jose Rivera, a twenty-one-year-old waiter who had come to New York from Puerto Rico just a year earlier. Clinton had taken out life insurance and accident insurance policies worth $7,000 on his purported brother and offered another man $5,000 to help do away with Rivera. That man informed the district attorney of the plot, however, and the case was reopened, leading to Glinton's arrest.[339]

This was the first case of insurance homicide in New York City since 1941 and recalled a notorious 1933 case involving Michael Malloy a.k.a. Iron

Postcard for Hotel Marie Antoinette, early twentieth century. *The Miriam and Ira D. Wallach Division of Art, Prints and Photographs: Picture Collection, The New York Public Library. "Hotel Marie Antoinette, New York City, N.Y." New York Public Library Digital Collections. Accessed March 27, 2020. http://digitalcollections.nypl.org/items/510d47e2-8cb3-a3d9-e040-e00a18064a99.*

Mike a.k.a. the Indestructible Man. Nine attempts were made on Malloy's life by five men trying to collect $2,000 in life insurance. The tenth attempt succeeded, but the men were caught, with four of them eventually executed at Sing Sing.[340]

THE POSTAL CLERK

It was understandable why Lawrence Skelson wanted to make a little more money. By September 1958, the postal clerk had been employed by the Pennsylvania Railroad for twenty-five years, having worked his annual salary up to $7,200 (about $65,000 today). But the fifty-year-old man who lived in the Bronx was the father of seven children, so there was likely little left over after paying all the bills. For the past seven years, Skelson had supplemented his salary by serving as the treasurer of the railroad's credit union, a part-time job that paid $1,000 a year.[341]

Just like every workday morning for the past quarter century, Skelson made his way to his office in Pennsylvania Terminal between 7th and 8th Avenues and West 31st and West 33rd Streets. Unexpectedly, Skelson excused himself from a group of colleagues to go to a washroom. Seconds later, a shot echoed through the train station, and a porter found the man dead on the floor. Beside him was a .38-caliber revolver for which he had a permit as a postal worker. Also near him was a brief note written on a sheet of toilet paper: "I'm sorry."[342]

Interior of Pennsylvania Terminal. *Irma and Paul Milstein Division of United States History, Local History and Genealogy, The New York Public Library. "West 34th Street–Eighth Avenue" New York Public Library Digital Collections. Accessed March 27, 2020. http://digitalcollections.nypl.org/items/510d47e2-c309-a3d9-e040-e00a18064a99.*

An investigation revealed that the credit union's books were being audited by the State Banking Department. After Skelson's suicide, a spokesman for the department made it clear that the audit was routine and that no irregularities had yet been found. Still, police had been informed that certain "discrepancies" were present in the fund's records, prompting the state's audit.[343]

THE STATION AGENT

You might question his judgment, but you also have to respect his commitment to his job. Twice before, Clyde Vincent, a subway token seller at the IND station at West 110th Street and Central Park West, had fought off holdup men, and in December 1959, he took the same action. This time, however, the gunman shot Vincent dead when the station agent refused to give him any money. The fifty-seven-year-old, who had worked for the Transit Authority for twenty-seven years, was found dead in his booth from a .32-caliber bullet in his chest. The bullet was embedded in the rear of the booth, and the shell case lay about ten feet away.[344]

No fewer than fifty detectives were assigned to the case, and they were all searching for the weapon and possible witnesses in hopes either could lead to the killer, who had not earned a dime for his crime.[345]

5

THE 1960s

Manhattan in the early 1960s picked up much like where the 1950s left off. Dinner and a floorshow were staples of classy entertainment. Eddie Fisher, Harry Belafonte and Phyllis Diller were regular headliners at the Royal Box at the Americana Hotel, while Nat King Cole, Jimmy Durante, Lena Horne or Jerry Lewis might be performing at the Copacabana on any given night. Sammy Davis Jr. and Liberace frequently held court at the Latin Quarter, and one had a decent chance of seeing Frank Sinatra, Judy Garland or Ethel Merman gathered around Jilly's piano bar just for fun.

Like that of entertainment, the culinary landscape of Manhattan in the 1960s would today be quite unfamiliar. Shrafft's had more than twenty locations, and there were twenty-six Horn & Hardart Automats, each place beloved by New Yorkers and visitors for their decent food at a decent price. With some thirty locations, Chock Full O'Nuts was the Starbucks of its day, serving up cups of joe for ten cents and doughnuts for a dime as well (no tipping please). A very nice dinner could be had in the city for five dollars and, for ten, a full meal at fine restaurants like the Oak Room or Sardi's.

Business types also gravitated toward the Playboy Club and its herd of buxom women in bunny outfits. Two-fisted drinkers were partial to the Club Car at the Hotel Roosevelt; the bar designed like a train car was just the place for a quick bump before getting on the train to Westchester or Connecticut (especially because the place had no seats). Toots Shor was the place to gawk at famous athletes drinking and smoking like there was

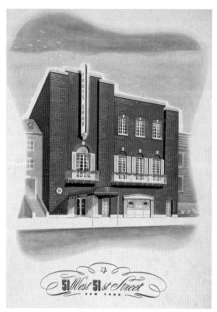 

Left: Menu for the Toots Shor Restaurant, a second home for many celebrities from the 1940s to 1960s. *Rare Book Division, The New York Public Library. "Toots Shor" New York Public Library Digital Collections. Accessed March 27, 2020. http://digitalcollections.nypl.org/items/ b1b72a60-9516-52d5-e040-e00a1806497a.*

Right: Menu for the Oak Room, the iconic restaurant and bar at the Plaza Hotel. *Rare Book Division, The New York Public Library. "Oak Room" New York Public Library Digital Collections. Accessed March 27, 2020. http://digitalcollections.nypl.org/items/b0d65bdd-77d1-7d0a-e040- e00a18065084.*

no tomorrow. Manhattanites were positively Polynesian-happy in the mid-1960s. Trader Vics (in the bowels of the Plaza Hotel), Hawaii Kai, Luau 400 and the Hawaiian Room at the Hotel Lexington were all places to get some mighty strong drinks with paper umbrellas.

Despite the good times, many New Yorkers could sense the cultural storm that was rapidly approaching in the mid-1960s. Cracks in the city's foundation were becoming too large to simply ignore, cracks that were threatening the golden age in which many Manhattanites had achieved unprecedented prosperity. Along with these fractures, which were dividing New Yorkers along political, social and economic lines, a growing sense of cynicism and disillusionment was palpable in the air. The Camelot days of Manhattan were rapidly fading, increasing the chances that a resident or visitor to the island would end up dead on arrival.

POOR COORDINATION

Did the October 1961 death of Allison Montague, Columbia University's psychiatric adviser for students and a staff member of St. Luke's Hospital, have anything to do with the spill he had taken the day before? Further investigation was needed to solve the curious case.[346]

What was known was that the forty-seven-year-old man was dead in his apartment on Riverside Drive near West 100th Street. A part-time maid discovered his body, although he was alive when she arrived at the apartment at 9:00 a.m. Still, there was reason to be concerned about the psychiatrist's condition. He had a bandage on his head, and blood was splattered around the apartment, including on the living room walls, the bathroom sink, his bedclothes and the floor. When the maid inquired about the source of the blood, Montague said it was that of his sick dog. (The police learned later that the dog had died about six weeks earlier.) Around 11:00 a.m., the maid heard a thud, and Montague was dead on the floor.[347]

Police backtracked to the day before to shed more light on the strange situation. Montague had walked into the emergency room at Roosevelt Hospital at 6:25 a.m. for treatment of a scalp wound that he said he received in a fall in his apartment after taking phenobarbital pills. After getting six stitches, he was released and went to his office as usual. This was not the first time Montague had fallen and injured himself after taking the sedative, a friend of the man's told police.[348] He was in fact known to have "poor coordination," and the police concluded that the bloodstains in his apartment were from the injury to his head after falling. An autopsy revealed that cause of death was the result of a chemical that had been self-administered, putting an end to the weird case.[349]

FUNERAL ARRANGEMENTS

Morris Weingarten had a plan, and he stuck to it. In September 1961, the sixty-seven-year-old man from Miami Beach came to New York and paid a visit to the Riverside Memorial Chapel on the Upper West Side. After making his funeral arrangements, he paid for a burial plot in the New York City area.[350]

A month later, Weingarten sent a letter to a friend in the Bronx, asking him to take care of his belongings if his body was found. Knowing Weingarten was staying at the Governor Clinton Hotel, his friend rushed over to his room. Weingarten was dead in a tub of water, an apparent suicide, and his body was sent to the Bellevue Hospital morgue.[351]

A TRIP AROUND THE WORLD

She had sold her house, and she was looking forward to a trip around the world that would begin in a couple of weeks. But it was not to be for Esther Kesselman, a widow from White Plains, New York, who checked into the Hotel Park Royal on West 73rd Street in April 1962. The fifty-six-year-old woman was found dead in her room, strangled and with a fractured skull.[352]

Although Kesselman—whose husband, a real estate dealer, had died a few years earlier and left her wealthy—had obviously died violently, her room was orderly and there were no signs of a struggle. Also, the door to the hotel room was locked, making police wonder how the murderer got in and out. Was the motive robbery? It wasn't clear. A checkbook revealed "a substantial balance," not surprising given her house netted $75,000 (ten times that today), but she had just $2 in her pocketbook, along with some jewelry. Thirty detectives, led by Assistant Chief Inspector Edward Byrnes, were on the case, beginning by interviewing the dead woman's two sisters to determine if the killer might have been someone she knew.[353]

THE DOLL MAN

The sidewalk peddler of dancing paper dolls was a well-known figure in Times Square. His name was Clarence Ritchie, and he sold his dolls on Broadway between West 46th and West 47th Streets. The dolls, made of crepe paper, appeared to dance on their own, but there was of course a trick. The seller, or a partner nearby, would pull on a nearly invisible string, amazing the crowds that gathered day and night in the area. The dolls cost one dollar.[354]

One night in September 1964, Ritchie was as usual demonstrating his dancing dolls to a mostly fascinated group of people. Abruptly, a man in the crowd began shouting that the demonstration was a fake, and he kicked at the string that was manipulating the dolls. Ritchie reacted by calling the man, Peter Droner, an obscene name; Droner then repeated that the show was a fraud. Ritchie then punched Droner, an investigator for the Transit Authority and a decorated ex-cop, in the jaw, sending him backward. Droner responded by drawing his .38 police revolver, for which he had a permit, and firing three shots, all of which hit Ritchie in the chest. Droner fled the scene, heading north on Broadway, but the doll peddler was dead on arrival at Roosevelt Hospital.[355]

The shooting happened to be shortly before curtain time at theaters, and soon thousands of people gravitated to the spot to see what had happened. Traffic was jammed in all directions for blocks, and some climbed on top of the unmoving cars to get a better view. Ten mounted policemen soon arrived along with half a dozen squad cars to try to clear the area. Meanwhile, two officers in a police car had nabbed Droner, and he confessed to the crime at the West 47th Street station house.[356]

A MANNISH HAIRCUT

The young woman who walked into Harlem Hospital at 5:00 a.m. one day in January 1966 was hurt and needed medical care. She had injured her left arm in an elevator door, she told a doctor. Meanwhile, detectives in an adjoining room were watching other doctors pronounce a man dead on arrival. He was found slumped over the steering wheel of a taxi at West 141st Street and Edgecombe Avenue.[357]

Two isolated events? Not at all. In examining the woman, who was dressed in dungarees and a black parka and had "a mannish haircut," Dr. Gladstone Hodge determined that her wound came from a gunshot rather than an elevator door. The dead man in the next room, a seventy-seven-year-old cabdriver named Martin Seiler, had a gunshot through his throat, leading the detectives to put two and two together. After being treated, the woman was questioned at the West 135th Street station, and she admitted shooting the cabdriver while robbing him. She had placed her left arm around the victim's neck and was wounded when the bullet from her .22-caliber derringer pistol passed through his neck.[358]

The woman's gun was found in her apartment, and police were seeking a possible accomplice. Seiler had driven his taxi in the city for the past forty-one years, most of it at night.[359]

THE DETECTIVE

A detective was dead in February 1966, something that makes other detectives very concerned. Lieutenant Edward Drum, who led the detective squad in the East New York section in Brooklyn, died after being in a fight with two men outside the Copacabana nightclub on East 60th Street. It wasn't clear how the fifty-two-year-old man died, but the district attorney's office was determined to get at the bottom of it.[360]

The first fact gathered was that Drum, who'd been on the force for twenty-five years, had been drinking with the two men at the club for a couple of hours prior to the fight. One of the men was Harry Sperling, a shipping executive, the other James Branigan Jr., an attorney. The men arrived at the club with Drum, who was off duty at the time (1:30 a.m.), and after a few cocktails they left together. It was then that the fight appeared to have taken place. Sperling and Branigan were naturally brought in for questioning, but no charges were filed by the DA, as more evidence had to be gathered. A report from the medical examiner's office would go a long way toward determining Drum's cause of death, specifically whether it was due to homicide or to something else.[361]

An autopsy of the man was fast-tracked, and it showed that the detective had died of a fractured skull and contusions of the brain. The three men got along while drinking, the manager of the Copa told police, but the situation had clearly changed when they got outside at 3:30 a.m.[362] Drum's head had been severely battered, meaning it was a case of homicide. Any number of things—being kicked in the face, getting stomped on, having one's head smashed repeatedly against a wall, receiving numerous blows by a blunt instrument or fists or simply falling down hard—could have caused the injuries, according to Deputy Chief Medical Examiner John Devlin. Drum had suffered no injuries on any other part of his body, he noted, something rather unusual in such cases.[363]

While no arrests had yet been made, subpoenas were issued to Sperling, Branigan and a number of other people. There was no doubt there had been a street fight, but much else about the case remained unknown. Determining whether the homicide was excusable, justifiable or criminal was key. The district attorney was hoping that appearances before a grand jury in two weeks would provide the answers.[364]

Menu for the Copacabana, the legendary Manhattan nightclub. *Rare Book Division, The New York Public Library. "Monte Proser's Copacabana" New York Public Library Digital Collections. Accessed March 27, 2020. http://digitalcollections.nypl.org/items/b7ece31d-7f5d-8808-e040-e00a18063f2c.*

THE DENTIST

One morning in October 1967, a patient arrived at his dentist's office on Broadway near West 39th Street. He was likely not looking forward to having two teeth pulled by Dr. Arthur Klein, but what he saw when he entered his office was even more upsetting. Klein's office had been ransacked, and the dentist was lying face-down in the anteroom of the three-room suite. He was bound hand and foot and dead.[365]

Police Inspector Seymour Silver examined the scene and Klein's body. The dentist's hands were tied with his own necktie, and his ankles were bound with a telephone cord that had been cut. No wounds were found on his body, however, leading the inspector to believe that Klein had died of a heart attack caused by the trauma. The man had a history of heart trouble, it was learned, making this a reasonable conclusion. Burglaries were not uncommon in the building, tenants told Silver, and Klein was known for offering his services at no charge to narcotics addicts.[366]

MUTED SCREAMS

Was it really an "apparent suicide," as the assistant medical examiner ruled in July 1968 after examining the body of Judith Rose? The twenty-three-year-old, a secretary for a publisher, was found shot dead by a rifle in her apartment on East 6th Street. Rose was discovered lying face-up on the floor of her bedroom. She was shot once in the chest, and a .22-caliber rifle was on the bed, just an arm's length from her body. She'd been married just three weeks.[367]

Rose was quite a bit more than a secretary, however, making her death that much more unfortunate. She and her husband, Donald, were active members of the East Sixth Street Block Association, helping to improve the neighborhood, which some considered to be a "slum." The couple painted the exteriors of buildings and local stores, often using a flower motif. They also helped clear an empty lot and convert it into a playground for the neighborhood's children.[368]

The medical examiner's declaration was curious given what Rose's downstairs neighbor told police when they investigated the death. She said she heard "muted screams" before the rifle shot, shrieks that "sounded as if somebody who wanted to scream was being strangled."

Shooting oneself in the chest with a rifle is possible but not easy, reason to look into the matter further. Police were questioning her husband, a city welfare investigator.[369]

THE COED

The tumultuous 1968 Democratic National Convention had been held in Chicago just a few days earlier, and Senator Eugene McCarthy finished well behind Vice President Hubert Humphrey in nomination votes on the first ballot. It was clear that McCarthy would not be the Democratic candidate in the upcoming presidential election, something that was too much to bear for twenty-two-year-old Minna Gross.[370]

In late August 1968, the body of the Columbia University "coed," as she was described in newspaper reports, was found in her room at the International House on Riverside Drive near West 122nd Street. An empty pill bottle was at Gross's side, and she left a note explaining that she was depressed over McCarthy's defeat at the convention. She was "a brilliant student," friends said, and made it known that she was against America's involvement in the Vietnam War. Columbia was a hotbed of student activism at the time, of course, and Gross had taken part in several antiwar demonstrations along with other college students.[371]

THE UNRULY RIDER

Crosby Littlejohn had been arrested thirty-five times, including three for assaulting a transit policeman, but his run ended in March 1969 in a subway car at 86th Street and Lexington Avenue. The police received a report that there was an unruly rider on one of its trains, and Patrolman Michael Sullivan reported to the scene. Littlejohn was indeed threatening and insulting the twenty-five passengers in the car and using language that was most alarming.[372]

Sullivan confronted the fifty-year-old man, and soon the two were in a struggle. In the tussle, Littlejohn somehow caused Sullivan's pistol, which was in his holster, to go off, wounding the policeman in the leg. Perhaps not knowing if Littlejohn had fired a shot with his own gun, Sullivan then fired three times at Littlejohn, and the man was dead. The passengers watched the ugly scene in stunned silence.[373]

CHARMING AND URBANE

The bank executive was late to a meeting one day in August 1969, which was unlike him—so unlike Lincoln Noblet in fact that the bank, First National City, sent a security officer to his apartment building on East 85th Street at 1st Avenue. When the security officer wasn't able to enter Noblet's duplex, he called the police, which turned out to save some time. The forty-two-year-old man was dead, having been severely beaten, although he may also have been stabbed, given that the apartment was, in the words of police, a "bloody mess."[374]

Described by a colleague as "charming and urbane," Noblet reportedly shared the apartment with a friend who was currently out of the country. Police were exploring the possibility that robbery was the motive for the slaying, as they had little idea who would want to kill the well-dressed confirmed bachelor.[375]

NOTES

1. The 1920s

1. "Found Dead after 'Loss of $2,000,000'," *New York Times*, October 10, 1920, 16.
2. Ibid.
3. "Visit to Former Wife Ends in Death," *New York Times*, May 7, 1921, 11.
4. Ibid.
5. "Collins Set Hour for His Suicide," *New York Times*, May 24, 1921, 5.
6. Ibid.
7. "Knife Is Driven Through His Body," *New York Times*, May 27, 1921, 23.
8. Ibid.
9. "Woman Murdered and Robbed in Flat," *New York Times*, June 18, 1921, 5.
10. Ibid.
11. "Woman Murdered in Home with Towel," *New York Times*, July 2, 1921, 5.
12. Ibid.
13. "Doctor's Ex-Wife, in Debt, Ends Life," *New York Times*, August 28, 1921, 10.
14. Ibid.
15. "Slain on His Wedding Day," *New York Times*, November 8, 1921, 12.
16. Ibid.
17. "Japanese Killed in Feud," *New York Times*, March 22, 1922, 2.
18. Ibid.
19. "Dr. F.A. Roy Kills Himself in Rooms," *New York Times*, May 11, 1922, 11.
20. Ibid.
21. Ibid.

22. "Find Woman Slain By an Alarm Clock," *New York Times*, August 6, 1922, 14.

23. Ibid.

24. Ibid.

25. "Husband Arrested for Clock Murder," *New York Times*, August 7, 1922, 2.

26. "Kills His Wife; Stabs Himself Ten Times," *New York Times*, September 1, 1922, 11.

27. Ibid.

28. "Find Model Dead, Her Jewels Gone," *New York Times*, March 16, 1923, 3.

29. "Murder of Model Not Part of Plot," *New York Times*, March 20, 1923, 4.

30. "Youth Shot Dead at Synagogue Door," *New York Times*, August 11, 1923, 11.

31. Ibid.

32. "Inventor a Suicide in a Rifle Gallery," *New York Times*, April 16, 1924, 16.

33. Ibid.

34. "Follies Girl Dies in Her Bathtub," *New York Times*, August 17, 1924, 9.

35. "Follies Girl's Death Shorn of Mystery," *New York Times*, August 18, 1924, 15.

36. "Kills Himself in Opera House Studio Home; Note Says Only Good Thing Left Is a Prelude," *New York Times*, September 5, 1925, 5.

37. Ibid.

38. "Gangster Is Slain; Shot from Ambush," *New York Times*, September 8, 1925, 23.

39. Ibid.

40. "Slain with Shovel After Bullets Fail," *New York Times*, January 24, 1926, 5.

41. Ibid.

42. "East Side Hunts Missing 'Kibitzer,'" *New York Times*, February 8, 1926, 21.

43. Ibid.

44. "Organizer Is Slain, Thrown into Street," *New York Times*, May 19, 1926, 27.

45. Ibid.

46. "Cat Saves 8 Lives, But Loses Its Own," *New York Times*, April 21, 1927, 18.

47. Ibid.

48. "One Slain in Street in a Pistol Fight," *New York Times*, April 29, 1927, 24.

49. Ibid.

50. "Man Killed in Club in Fight Over Steak," *New York Times*, July 20, 1927, 9.

51. Ibid.

52. "Suicide 'Poetic,' Girl Dies by Gas," *New York Times*, July 30, 1927, 17.

53. Ibid.

54. Ibid.

55. "Motorist Is Slain Aiding Police Chase," *New York Times*, August 15, 1927, 19.

56. Ibid.

57. Ibid.

58. Ibid.

59. "Says Victim of Blast Made Bomb Himself," *New York Times*, October 11, 1927, 31.

60. Ibid.

61. "Find Ex-Actress and Navy Man Dead," *New York Times*, December 26, 1927, 2.

62. "Sift Death of Two in Flat," *New York Times*, December 27, 1927, 11.

63. "Village 'Mayoress' Dies by Gas in Room," *New York Times*, February 14, 1928, 8.

64. Ibid.

65. Ibid.

66. "Body Bound in Bed; Suicide, Police Say," *New York Times*, July 5, 1928, 28.

67. Ibid.

68. "Woman Found Dead, Foul Play Suspected," *New York Times*, July 18, 1928, 10.

69. Ibid.

70. "Kills Girl Student and Ends Own Life," *New York Times*, March 14, 1929, 22.

71. Ibid.

72. Ibid.

73. "Jeweler Ends Life as Result of Theft," *New York Times*, May 14, 1929, 30.

74. Ibid.

75. "Find Clothier Shot in Hotel Olcott," *New York Times*, June 4, 1929, 20.

76. Ibid.

77. "Bashwitz Manager Is Held for Theft," *New York Times*, June 22, 1929, 2.

78. "Slays Café Owner, Then Ends Own Life," *New York Times*, August 5, 1929, 24.

79. Ibid.

80. "Dreading the Chair, Fugitive Ends Life," *New York Times*, August 15, 1929, 4.

81. Ibid.

82. "Private Detective Slain in Harlem," *New York Times*, August 28, 1929, 21.

83. Ibid.

84. "Fail to Find Clue in Gang Killing," *New York Times*, September 14, 1929, 12.

85. Ibid.

86. "Wealthy Youth Dies in Eight-Story Fall," *New York Times*, September 23, 1929, 1.

87. Ibid.

88. "Boy, 12, Confesses Strangling Woman," *New York Times*, October 25, 1929, 28.

89. Ibid.

90. Ibid.

91. "Telegram Reveals Slaying of Woman," *New York Times*, November 20, 1929, 3.

92. Ibid.

93. Ibid.

94. "Identifies Women Who Died in Hotel," *New York Times*, December 29, 1929, 21.

95. Ibid.

2. The 1930s

96. "Showgirl Ends Life in Architect's Home," *New York Times*, January 30, 1930, 18.
97. Ibid.
98. Ibid.
99. Ibid.
100. "Friend Refuses Aid, Is Shot Down in Row," *New York Times*, March 24, 1930, 13.
101. Ibid.
102. Ibid.
103. "Woman Ends Life; Brooded Over Play," *New York Times*, April 1, 1930, 15.
104. Ibid.
105. "Ends Life by Fumes in Auto on 213th St.," *New York Times*, September 12, 1930, 18.
106. Ibid.
107. "East Side 'Bad Man' Slain in Night Club," *New York Times*, November 1, 1930, 20.
108. Ibid.
109. Ibid.
110. "Dismembered Body of Man Is Found," *New York Times*, November 25, 1930, 56.
111. Ibid.
112. Ibid.
113. "Shot Dead by Friend in Speakeasy Row," *New York Times*, December 6, 1930, 12.
114. Ibid.
115. "Couple Shot Dead in Hotel Room Here," *New York Times*, January 25, 1931, 27.
116. Ibid.
117. "Parrot's Cry Leads to Murder Charge," *New York Times*, January 26, 1931, 6.
118. Ibid.
119. "Organ Grinder Dies with Wrists Bound," *New York Times*, February 4, 1931, 6.
120. Ibid.
121. "Dancer Kills Wife in Lawyer's Office," *New York Times*, May 3, 1931, 3.
122. Ibid.
123. Ibid.
124. Ibid.
125. "Editorial Writer, 79, Ends Life by Shot," *New York Times*, July 15, 1931, 21.
126. Ibid.
127. "Girl Slain After Liquor Party," *New York Times*, September 8, 1931, 52.
128. Ibid.
129. Ibid.
130. "Bootlegger Killed in Crowded Street," *New York Times*, September 15, 1931, 16.

131. Ibid.

132. "Undertaker's Aide Murdered in Shop," *New York Times*, October 4, 1931, 20.

133. Ibid.

134. "Two Stage Girls Die in Suicide Compact," *New York Times*, November 27, 1931, 26.

135. Ibid.

136. Ibid.

137. "Money Lost in Market; Ends Life with Rifle," *New York Times*, January 7, 1932, 3.

138. Ibid.

139. Ibid.

140. "Ends Life Surrounded by Playing Children," *New York Times*, February 27, 1932, 5.

141. Ibid.

142. Ibid.

143. "Woman Shot Dead; Husband Is Missing," *New York Times*, March 4, 1932, 13.

144. Ibid.

145. Ibid.

146. "Woman of 60 Is Killed by Thief in Tenement," *New York Times*, April 1, 1932, 22.

147. Ibid.

148. "Suicide Identified as Ex-Aide of Capone," *New York Times*, August 2, 1932, 34.

149. Ibid.

150. Ibid.

151. "Chauffer Is Slain Near Walker Home," *New York Times*, September 3, 1932, 28.

152. Ibid.

153. "Woman Found Shot Had Told of Threat," *New York Times*, October 5, 1932, 46.

154. Ibid.

155. "Son of Gen Haskell Is Found Shot Dead," *New York Times*, October 13, 1932, 3.

156. Ibid.

157. Ibid.

158. Ibid.

159. "Father Killed Trying to Hide Death of Pet; New Canary Bought for Son Leads to Fall," *New York Times*, October 20, 1932, 3.

160. Ibid.

161. Ibid.

162. "Dies with Legatee in Gas-Filled Room," *New York Times*, November 29, 1932, 10.

163. Ibid.

164. Ibid.

165. "Police Hunt Fails to Find Slayer," *New York Times*, January 3, 1933, 48.

166. Ibid.

167. "Shot Dead by Wife in Tudor City Home," *New York Times*, January 13, 1933, 36.

168. Ibid.

169. "Slayer of Husband Freed," *New York Times*, July 28, 1936, 11.

170. "Girl Points Out 3 as Slayers on Drive," *New York Times*, March 22, 1934, 14.

171. Ibid.

172. "Chinatown Leader Slain in His Office," *New York Times*, October 15, 1934, 38.

173. Ibid.

174. Ibid.

175. Ibid.

176. "Girl, 17, and Man Seized in Hold-Ups," *New York Times*, January 7, 1935, 36.

177. Ibid.

178. Ibid.

179. "Steinmetz Story of Slayings Read," *New York Times*, May 21, 1935, 40.

180. Ibid.

181. Ibid.

182. "Merchant Kills Himself," *New York Times*, May 23, 1935, 6.

183. Ibid.

184. "Missing Jeweler Found Murdered," *New York Times*, December 12, 1934, 2.

185. Ibid.

186. Ibid.

187. "One Dead, 2 Hurt in Peddlers' Row," *New York Times*, December 30, 1934, 3.

188. Ibid.

189. "Hotel Guest Kills House Detective," *New York Times*, January 29, 1935, 18.

190. Ibid.

191. "Prelude to Suicide Is Dinner with Kin," *New York Times*, April 25, 1935, 15.

192. Ibid.

193. Ibid.

194. Meyer Berger, "Gang War Bullets Thin Butler Clan," *New York Times*, March 16, 1936, 3.

195. Ibid.

196. "LaGuardia Rushes to Harlem Killing," *New York Times*, July 14, 1936, 15.

197. Ibid.

198. Ibid.

199. "Aide of Lucania Is Victim of Gang," *New York Times*, August 8, 1936, 28.

200. Ibid.

201. "Ex-Banker Slain in Basement Room," *New York Times*, June 11, 1937, 24.

202. Ibid.

203. Ibid.

204. "Convict on Parole Found Dead of Shot," *New York Times*, July 22, 1937, 27.

205. Ibid.

206. "Hangs Himself in Jail after $25,000 Thefts," *New York Times*, August 11, 1937, 42.

207. Ibid.

208. "Theatre Man Ends Life with Pistol," *New York Times*, November 6, 1937, 15.

209. Ibid.

210. Ibid.

211. "Ex-Publisher Dies; Inquiry Is Started," *New York Times*, November 26, 1937, 42.

212. Ibid.

213. Ibid.

214. "Man Held in Death of Woman Swimmer," *New York Times*, February 9, 1938, 14.

215. Ibid.

216. "Witness in Killing Plunges to Death," *New York Times*, April 14, 1938, 12.

217. Ibid.

218. "Suspect Found Dead," *New York Times*, April 27, 1938, 5.

219. Ibid.

220. "Broadcaster Ends Life by Gas in Home," *New York Times*, May 23, 1938, 7.

221. Ibid.

222. "Eviction Near, Ends Life," *New York Times*, May 24, 1938, 42.

223. Ibid.

224. "Irene Racz, Artist, Ends Life By Poison," *New York Times*, August 23, 1938, 38.

225. Ibid.

226. "Educator and Wife Die in 19-Story Fall," *New York Times*, September 24, 1938, 38.

227. Ibid.

228. "Refugee a Suicide with Her Husband," *New York Times*, December 6, 1938, 12.

229. Ibid.

230. Ibid.

231. "1 Killed, 3 Seized in Robbery Flurry," *New York Times*, December 23, 1938, 4.

232. Ibid.

233. "Café Racket Chief Is Found Shot Dead," *New York Times*, September 22, 1939, 28.

234. Ibid.

235. Ibid.

236. "Counterfeiter Slain in Tenement Hall," *New York Times*, November 30, 1939, 44.

237. Ibid.

238. Ibid.

3. The 1940s

239. "Mrs. H.D. Meredith Ends Life with Gas," *New York Times*, April 14, 1940, 21.
240. Ibid.
241. "Ex-Convict Slain; 3d Brother to Die," *New York Times*, August 27, 1940, 23.
242. Ibid.
243. "Electrical Pioneer Dies in Laboratory," *New York Times*, April 8, 1941, 27.
244. Ibid.
245. "Vesta Kelling, Writer, Dies in Gas Explosion; Death of Ex-Husband in Lisbon Also Reported," *New York Times*, December 4, 1941, 19.
246. Ibid.
247. "Woman, 52, Is Slain in Suite at Hotel," *New York Times*, March 6, 1942, 23.
248. Ibid.
249. Ibid.
250. Ibid.
251. "Lack of Doctor on Ambulance Delays Removal of Body in Gas Suicide Case," *New York Times*, March 28, 1942, 19.
252. Ibid.
253. "Bridegroom Found Dead in Auto Pit," *New York Times*, April 29, 1942, 22.
254. Ibid.
255. "Slain in Barber Chair as He Gets a Shave," *New York Times*, July 16, 1942, 2.
256. Ibid.
257. "Bride-To-Be Ends Life," *New York Times*, September 30, 1942, 25.
258. Ibid.
259. "Warden Found Dead in Air Raid Quarters," *New York Times*, October 2, 1942, 16.
260. Ibid.
261. "Park Death Case Called Homicide," *New York Times*, November 4, 1942, 25.
262. Ibid.
263. "Fish Handler Slain," *New York Times*, December 25, 1942, 12.
264. Ibid.
265. "Body Identified as Thief's," *New York Times*, January 16, 1943, 15.
266. Ibid.
267. "Fireman Found Dead in Doorway of Store," *New York Times*, September 15, 1943, 19.
268. Ibid.
269. "Pickpocket Subway Is Killed by a Train as He Flees Along Tracks Under Broadway," *New York Times*, January 20, 1944, 21.
270. Ibid.
271. "Dancer Found Dead with Mouth Taped," *New York Times*, February 8, 1944, 17.

272. Ibid.

273. "Woman Found Beaten, Strangled in Bushes at Planetarium Entrance," *New York Times*, August 26, 1944, 13.

274. Ibid.

275. "Scan Address Book for Murder Clues," *New York Times*, August 31, 1944, 18.

276. "Penthouse Death Linked to Robbery," *New York Times*, November 14, 1944, 25.

277. Ibid.

278. Ibid.

279. "Slain in Funeral Parlor," *New York Times*, December 14, 1944, 25.

280. Ibid.

281. "Blind Student Found Dead at Columbia," *New York Times*, January 28, 1945, 29.

282. Ibid.

283. Ibid.

284. "Elevator Murder East Side Mystery," *New York Times*, March 7, 1945, 23.

285. Ibid.

286. Ibid.

287. "Soldier Is Slain in Y.M.C.A. Hotel," *New York Times*, October 3, 1945, 21.

288. Ibid.

289. Ibid.

290. "Navy Officer Found Dead in Hotel Room, Woman Marine Companion Unconscious," *New York Times*, October 8, 1945, 14.

291. Ibid.

292. "Liquor Shop Owner Found Shot Dead," *New York Times*, January 16, 1946, 28.

293. Ibid.

294. "Prisoner in Assault Case Is Shot Dead as He Runs at Detective with Knife Drawn," *New York Times*, January 30, 1946, 31.

295. Ibid.

296. "Another Veteran Shot Dead in Park," *New York Times*, July 6, 1946, 11.

297. Ibid.

298. Ibid.

299. "Woman, 67, Found Slashed to Death," *New York Times*, March 2, 1947, 46.

300. Ibid.

301. "Strangler Kills Former Actress," *New York Times*, July 10, 1947, 44.

302. Ibid.

303. Ibid.

304. "Pianist Is Found Dead," *New York Times*, March 25, 1948, 22.

305. Ibid.

306. "Greenwich Village Poet Dies by Hanging after Surviving 5-Story Suicide Plunge," *New York Times*, September 9, 1948, 56.

307. Ibid.

308. "Tailor, 67, Is Slain in Tenth St. Shop," *New York Times*, September 15, 1948, 64.

309. Ibid.

4. The 1950s

310. "Landlady, 65, Is Slain in Cluttered Home," *New York Times*, January 7, 1951, 28.

311. Ibid.

312. "Hairdresser Slain in Tenement Hall," *New York Times*, November 11, 1951, 72.

313. Ibid.

314. "Dress Man Is Slain by Shots at Home," *New York Times*, February 10, 1952, 66.

315. Ibid.

316. "Girl Shot in Columbia Office; Killer Strolls Away, Escape," *New York Times*, July 15, 1952, 1.

317. William M. Farrell, "Pseudo Scientist Confesses Girl's Murder at Columbia," *New York Times*, July 18, 1952, 1.

318. "Suit Planned in Slaying," *New York Times*, August 6, 1952, 29.

319. "Parcel Thief Slain by Police in Chase," *New York Times*, May 8, 1953, 18.

320. Ibid.

321. "Chinese Slain in Shop; Seaman Being Hunted," *New York Times*, September 22, 1953, 19.

322. Ibid.

323. Edith Evans Asbury, "2 Girls Twice Try Suicide; One Dies," *New York Times*, July 22, 1954, 24.

324. Ibid.

325. "Suspect in Theft Found Murdered," *New York Times*, January 31, 1955, 28.

326. Ibid.

327. "Soldier Kills Wife, Spares Daughter, 2," *New York Times*, January 14, 1956, 38.

328. Ibid.

329. Peter Kihss, "Aide of Seminary Hanged in Home," *New York Times*, September 11, 1956, 38.

330. Ibid.

331. Ibid.

332. "Death of Divorcee Termed Suspicious," *New York Times*, December 28, 1956, 27.

333. Ibid.

334. "Ex-Official of Oil Company Dead with Companion in Hotel Here," *New York Times*, August 18, 1957, 44.

335. Ibid.; "Mystery Shrouds Deaths in Hotel," *New York Times*, August 19, 1957, 27.

336. "Ex-Official of Oil Company Dead"; "Mystery Shrouds Deaths."

337. "Mystery Shrouds Deaths in Hotel."

338. "Police Charge 'Fake' Brother with Murdering for Insurance," *New York Times*, January 15, 1958, 31.

339. Ibid.

340. Ibid.

341. "Credit Union Aide Is a Suicide Here," *New York Times*, September 23, 1958, 67.

342. Ibid.

343. Ibid.

344. "IND Station Agent Murdered in Booth," *New York Times*, December 11, 1959, 65.

345. Ibid.

5. The 1960s

346. "Psychiatrist Dies a Day After Fall," *New York Times*, October 22, 1961, 57.

347. Ibid.

348. Ibid.

349. "Violence Ruled Out in Death of Doctor," *New York Times*, October 23, 1961, 15.

350. "Man Who Arranged Funeral Ends Life," *New York Times*, October 24, 1961, 24.

351. Ibid.

352. "White Plains Widow Is Found Slain Here," *New York Times*, April 16, 1962, 24.

353. Ibid.

354. "Peddler Is Slain; Ex-Officer Held," *New York Times*, September 17, 1964, 32.

355. Ibid.

356. Ibid.

357. "Wounded Woman Seized in Hospital as Cabby's Slayer," *New York Times*, January 14, 1966, 36.

358. Ibid.

359. Ibid.

360. Murray Schumach, "Off-Duty Detective Found Dead after Fight Outside Copacabana," *New York Times*, February 27, 1966, 29.

361. Ibid.

362. Ibid.

363. Martin Gansberg, "Death of Detective Outside Club Ruled 'Homicidal,'" *New York Times*, February 28, 1966, 19.

364. Ibid.

365. "Dentist Found Dead Following Robbery in Garment Center," *New York Times*, October 13, 1967, 18.

366. Ibid.

367. Martin Tolchin, "Bride Shot in East Village," *New York Times*, July 16, 1968, 32.

368. Ibid.

369. Ibid.

370. "A Columbia Coed Found Dead Here," *New York Times*, September 1, 1968, 39.

371. Ibid.

372. "Transit Policeman Kills Unruly Rider," *New York Times*, March 3, 1969, 7.

373. Ibid.

374. "Bank Executive Is Found Slain in His Upper East Side Duplex," *New York Times*, August 30, 1969, 45.

375. Ibid.

BIBLIOGRAPHY

Cannato, Vincent J. *The Ungovernable City: John Lindsay and His Struggle to Save New York*. New York: Basic Books, 2002.

Caro, Robert A. *The Power Broker: Robert Moses and the Fall of New York*. New York: Knopf, 1974.

Charyn, Jerome. *Gangsters and Gold Diggers: Old New York, the Jazz Age, and the Birth of Broadway*. New York: Da Capo Press, 2004.

Diehl, Lorraine B. *Over Here!: New York City During World War II*. Washington, D.C.: Smithsonian Books, 2010.

Ellis, Edward Robb. *The Epic of New York City: A Narrative History*. New York: Basic Books, 2004.

Ferrera, Eric. *A Guide to Gangsters, Murderers and Weirdos of New York City's Lower East Side*. Charleston, SC: The History Press, 2009.

Goldstein, Richard. *Helluva Town: The Story of New York City During World War II*. New York: Free Press, 2010.

Lewis, David Levering. *When Harlem Was in Vogue*. New York: Knopf, 1981.

Miller, Donald L. *Supreme City: How Jazz Age Manhattan Gave Birth to Modern America*. New York: Simon & Schuster, 2015.

Phillips-Fein, Kim. *Fear City: New York's Fiscal Crisis and the Rise of Austerity Politics*. New York: Metropolitan Books, 2017.

Samuel, Lawrence R. *The End of the Innocence: The 1964–1965 New York World's Fair*. Syracuse, NY: Syracuse University Press, 2007.

———. *New York City 1964: A Cultural History*. Jefferson, NC: McFarland, 2014.

————. *Tudor City: Manhattan's Historic Residential Enclave*. Charleston, SC: The History Press, 2019.

Stewart, Jules. *Gotham Rising: New York in the 1930s*. London: I.B. Tauris, 2016.

Strausbaugh, John. *Victory City: A History of New York and New Yorkers During World War II*. New York: Twelve, 2018.

Wakefield, Dan. *New York in the 50s*. New York: Houghton Mifflin, 1992.

Williams, Mason B. *City of Ambition: FDR, LaGuardia, and the Making of Modern New York*. New York: W.W. Norton, 2013.

Wilson, Earl. *Earl Wilson's New York*. New York: Simon and Schuster, 1964.

Woliver, Robbie. *Hoot! A Twenty-Five Year History of the Greenwich Village Music Scene*. New York: St. Martin's Press, 1984.

ABOUT THE AUTHOR

LAWRENCE R. SAMUEL is the founder of AmeriCulture, a Miami- and New York City–based consultancy dedicated to thought leadership relating to the past, present and future of American culture. He holds a PhD in American studies, an MA in English from the University of Minnesota and an MBA in marketing from the University of Georgia and was a Smithsonian Institution Fellow.

Larry writes the *Psychology Yesterday*, *Boomers 3.0* and *Future Trends* blogs for psychologytoday.com. His previous books include *The End of the Innocence: The 1964–1965 New York World's Fair* (2007), *New York City 1964: A Cultural History* (2014) and *Tudor City: Manhattan's Historic Residential Enclave* (2019).

Visit us at
www.historypress.com